D0991553

MACH II WITH YOUR HAIR ON FIRE

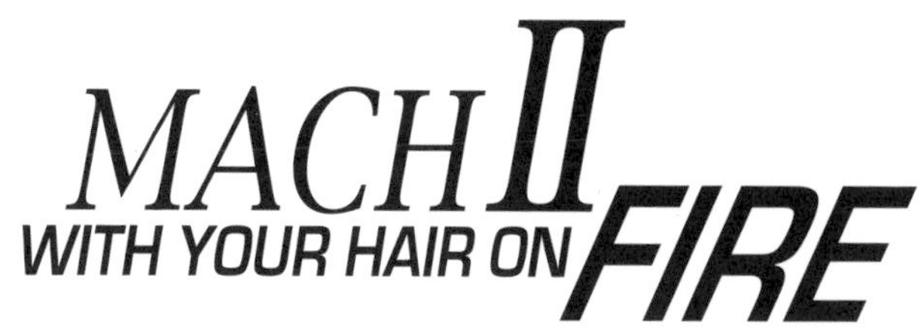

The Art of Vision and Self-Motivation

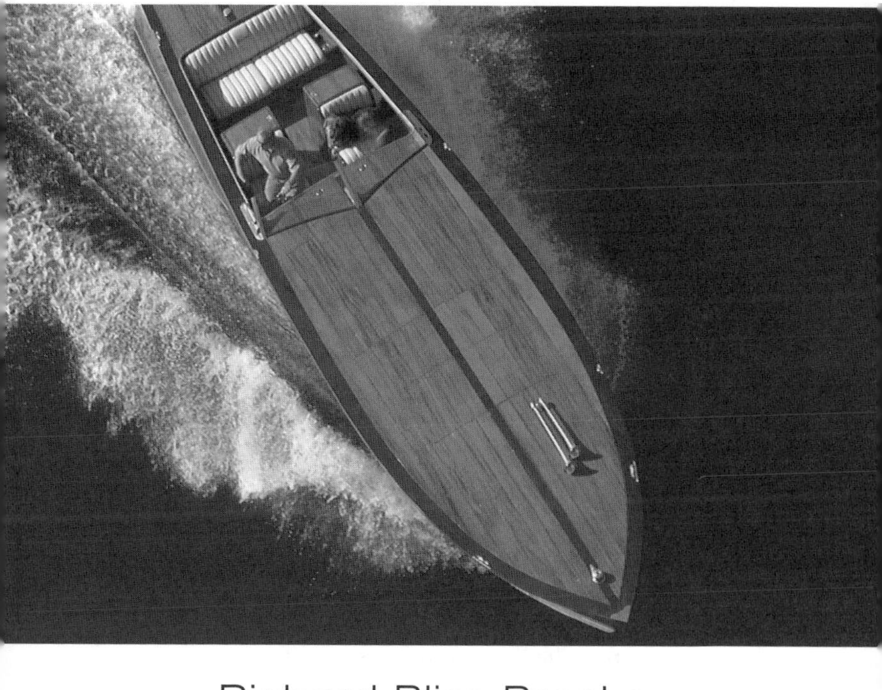

Richard Bliss Brooke

First edition published 2000
Second edition published 2001
Third edition published 2003
Fourth edition published 2004
Fifth edition hardcover published 2006
Sixth edition hardcover published 2008
Seventh edition hardcover published 2009
Eighth edition hardcover published 2011

ISBN # 0-970039-1-3
Published by High Performance People, L.L.C.
1875 North Lakewood Drive
Coeur d'Alene, ID 83814
Telephone (888) 665-8484, Fax (888) 665-8485

Printed in the United States of America

10 9 8 7 6 5 4 3 2 1

WHAT READERS ARE SAYING ABOUT *MACH II*

"Congratulations! Congratulations! Congratulations! Congratulations! Congratulations! I just read your *Mach II* book, and it is a masterpiece… head and shoulders above the rest of the motivation books I have read."

— Harvey Mackay
Chairman & Founder, MackayMitchell

"I love *Mach II With Your Hair On Fire*. I could tell when I read the book that Richard has a passion for changing people's lives. I respect Richard and his work and thank him for who he is and the difference and impact he's making in people's lives and businesses."

— Les Brown
Motivational Speaker

"If you are committed to extraordinary success, *Mach II* is a must-have for your personal library! The information on Vision and Self-Motivation is some of the best you will find anywhere. Thank you, Richard. You are a great example of what a person can do with the right information. Plus, you understand the importance of sharing."

— Bob Proctor
Author of the best-selling book, *You Were Born Rich*

"Many students of success write about it, second-hand. Richard Brooke, a master mentor, writes about success as he has experienced it. There is a life-altering gem of wisdom on every page. Read, internalize and positive change will materialize."

— DENIS WAITLEY
Author, *The Psychology of Winning*

"Richard Brooke's *Mach II* is a fast-moving, entertaining book full of fast, funny, helpful ideas on success and achievement."

— BRIAN TRACY
Author, *Goals!*

"In this accelerated economy you have to travel at *Mach II*. This book teaches you how to do it in an omni-effective and fun way."

— MARK VICTOR HANSEN
Co-creator, #1 *New York Times* best-selling series *Chicken Soup for the Soul* and Co-author, *The One Minute Millionaire*

"I found a copy of *Mach II* at a friend's house. I read and loved it. So much of what the great athletes do to accomplish the impossible is done through visualization. Richard captures exactly how it works, why it works, and how anyone can use it to do great things in their life. Richard has a unique way of telling the story so we all really get it! I highly recommend this book to anyone wanting to master their own motivation and accomplishments."

— JOHN ELWAY
Super Bowl MVP & NFL Hall of Fame Quarterback

"I can sincerely say that Richard Brooke has changed my way of thinking more than anyone. I will always be grateful to Richard for making me a better person."

— Gale Sayers
NFL Hall of Fame Running Back

"Before every game, I would visualize how I would react in different situations on the ice. *Mach II* will teach you how visualization can separate you from the rest and give you the edge needed to succeed."

— Adam Deadmarsh
2002 Olympic Silver Medalist, Hockey; Stanley Cup Winner, Colorado Avalanche; Stanley Cup Play-off MVP, Los Angeles Kings

"Richard Brooke's *Mach II* is extraordinary. I loved it."

— Dan Quayle
44th Vice President of the United States

"I loved *Mach II*. Richard captures the laws of attraction and action wonderfully. I am giving it to all my agents."

— John Beutler
#1 Agent in the world for Century 21, 2003 & 2005

"The number one thing I look for in people I come across in Network Marketing is integrity. Integrity is why Richard Brooke has become a legend in the Network Marketing field. Combine that with the fact that he is one of the few who has been successful both as a distributor in the field and an executive in the home office and you will see why Richard is regularly recognized by industry leaders as one of the best! Get his books, go to his seminars, subscribe to his newsletters. Get all you can from Richard!"

— Chris Widener

"I recommend *Mach II* to everyone. The book offers many points to ponder. One of my favorites is the distinction of knowing who you are and where you want to go in your life. You must DECIDE and ACT."

— Bill Morrow
Founder, The Quarry at LaQuinta & Branson Creek Golf Club

"Absolutely incredible!"

— John Addison
Co-CEO, Primerica

"Passion and a belief in each individual's potential seem to jump out of Richard Brooke's book. Reading it is both adventurous and a career map."

— Rick Goings
Chairman & CEO, Tupperware Brands Corporation;
Former President, Avon Germany and Avon USA

"I got a lot from *Mach II* and borrowed some of Richard's quotes for an offsite strategy session I facilitated. This book is so good that I ordered a few copies for my friends and family."

— Charles Orr
Former President, Shaklee Corporation

"*Mach II* is absolutely brilliant. I don't know a person in the world who wouldn't benefit from reading it and building a bigger vision, then manifesting it into their life!"

— Randy Gage
A pre-eminent expert on Network Marketing

"If vision is tomorrow's reality expressed as an idea today, then *Mach II* is a turbo charger into your new reality. I started reading and couldn't put it down until I was finished! Simply put, Richard Brooke's book will teach you how to unleash your imagination in the successful pursuit of your dreams."

— Orrin Woodward
Co-Author of *NY Times & Wall St. Journal* Best Seller - *Launching a Leadership Revolution*

"Touching and powerful, *Mach II* contributes Richard Brooke's greatest gift: an inspiring challenge to change the way we think about ourselves, life, and what's possible. A masterpiece."

— Russ DeVan
CEO, Success by Design, Inc.

"Warning: Be sure to put the car on cruise control when listening to Mach II, or be prepared to pay for a speeding ticket. The information will supercharge your business and your life!"

— Doug Cloward
President & Co-Founder, Heritage Makers

"Powerful! When Richard Brooke says it, you can believe it. He has lived it and he can guide the way to success. This is a 'must read' for all students in pursuit of excellence!"

— Kevin B. Young
Director of Sales, RBC Life Sciences

"I love this book! Richard Brooke has shown us how to own our destiny and author our own reality through the power of personal vision. When you finish this book, you will know that — no matter who you are or what you do — you are an artist. And, the masterpiece you are creating is your own life. Required reading."

— Sandy Elsberg
Author, *Bread Winner, Bread Baker*

"Vision is the cornerstone of all achievement. And Richard Brooke's *Mach II* is far and away the most clear, compelling, complete and immediately useful, results-getting work on vision ever written!"

— John Milton Fogg
Founder of Upline® & Network Marketing Lifestyles; Author of *The Greatest Networker in the World*, and *The Inner Game of Network Marketing*

"Richard Brooke is one of the finest men in the Network Marketing industry. He knows his stuff and produced *Mach II* with flying colors. I recommend this book and audio series to anyone who is committed to moving their business on the fast track."

— PEGGY LONG
Trainer, Coach & Author, *On This Rock*

"If you want to live a more wonderful life, and help others do so, then study and apply the brilliant wisdom in this short gem. The audio version of Richard's *Mach II,* plus the handy overview card for building one's vision, is a huge bonus, which makes this important resource invaluable."

— ART BURLEIGH
Double Diamond Executive, EYI

"Richard's work has impacted me in a major way, taking me higher and farther than I would have gone without it. I've passed it along and seen phenomenal results in people's lives and businesses. Thank you for *Mach II*!"

— PAUL DEVLIN
President, Exodus Marketing Group

"Richard Brooke captures the essence of success principle No. 1: You've got to believe it before you will see it. Through his own experiences, he comes to life in a brilliantly simple, thought-provoking, powerful message about developing a new belief system. He grabs you from page one. A handbook for anyone wanting to create a success mentality!"

— CAROL ANTON
Executive National Sales Director #4 Consultant
in the nation for Mary Kay Cosmetics

"Richard Brooke is the consummate mentor and storyteller, and Mach II can be the roadmap for changing your whole life! I enthusiastically recommend this compelling personal story that is sure to touch your heart and mind."

— Dave Johnson
31-year Network Marketing Veteran & Nikken Royal Ambassador

"Without a vision, the people perish. Get ready to craft that empowering vision for yourself, your team and your family. Focus on what's possible in people's lives and watch them achieve the extraordinary. Richard Brooke's *Mach II* has helped members of our global leadership team forge compelling visions, master their own motivation, and create tangible results at Mach II speed!"

— Art Jonak
Author, Speaker, Certified Network Marketing Professional & Founder, Network Professionals

"Richard Brooke is one of my favorite Masters of Network Marketing. Little did I know when I first received the *Mach II* manuscript in 1997 what a huge impact it would have on my life, both in business and personal. All these years later, his words are still invaluable to me!"

— Jackie Ulmer
Lake Arrowhead, CA

"*Mach II* was one of the first books I bought and read when I realized that my life was the product of my best thinking. If I wanted different results, I had to create them. Anyone who wants to create immediate results in any area of their life will find this book has a nuts-and-bolts approach that will work ... if you are willing to apply it."

— Tony Rush
Alabama

"Like its author, this book is a never-to-be-forgotten masterpiece on the art of how you really CAN have it all ... even despite great odds. Richard's word pictures will paint a landscape in your mind and heart that can trigger a huge new world of possibility for you. Using Richard's vision technology, we have generated over $10 million in Network Marketing income — and a 'pinch me' lifestyle on our own terms."

— Dr. Eileen Silva & Taylor Hegan
Southlake, TX

"I've been a student of Richard Brooke since 1995, when I was introduced to his work through a Vision Workshop. Hearing *Mach II* on audio is like reliving that workshop and getting the power of repetition and reinforcement. The first CD alone I listened to three times to get the strategies for creating a vision locked in, so I could pass them on to people I meet around the world. I will recommend *Mach II* as long as I have breath. In fact, I list Richard's website in my latest book, where I make it clear that without a vision we cannot create the life of our dreams."

— Mark "Google Superman" Davis
Public Speaker, Coach & Author, The Internet Success Secret

"Practical, real-life solutions for any sales professional. I have known and worked with Richard Brooke for more than 17 years, and he walks his talk. Everything we do in life requires clear vision and the discipline to stay motivated. I recommend *Mach II* to everyone I come into contact with who manages people."

— Scott Kufus
VP of Business Development, Genewize Life Sciences

"Richard Brooke is an articulate and powerful motivator. *Mach II* has substance, relevance and will make a positive difference in the lives of those wise enough to use its principles. Plus, it's a fun read."

— Rudy Revak
President & Founder, Symmetry Corporation

"I am of the opinion that it's the size of one's vision that determines the extent of one's courage. If you'd like to boldly go where you've never gone before, use Richard's book to take you there."

— John Kalench
Late Founder/President, Millionaires in Motion, Inc.

"I've read and reviewed most every book on personal development there is. I only give credence to books written by authors whose lives are a testimony to the principles they preach. I want to know the success principles that elevated someone from a chicken cutter earning $3.05 an hour to a multi-millionaire … and you will too! In *Mach II*, Richard shares timeless principles to help you find the courage, motivation and pathway to greater success."

— Darren Hardy
Publisher, SUCCESS magazine

"The example of Richard Brooke's dynamic, visionary leadership is what first awakened my interest in the field of Network Marketing. As his book makes clear, he's committed to inspiring people — even outside his great company."

— Scott DeGarmo
Author of *Heart to Heart* & former Editor-in-Chief, *SUCCESS* magazine

"Our work at Human Potential is intended to help companies shape their future. This involves work on values, vision, mission, strategy and generating the competence to implement them. Our clients include companies like Microsoft, Intel, EDS, CapitolOne and Amgen. *Mach II* is a must-read for anyone who wants to get it quickly, clearly and powerfully!"

— CHRIS MAJER
CEO, Human Potential Project

"Read *Mach II* vigilantly. Diligently practice what it says. Richard Brooke is an extraordinary leader who walks his talk … no simple feat. And what a great set of footprints to emulate!"

— CAROL MCCALL, PHD
Founder, The Institute for Global Listening & Communication

"As an executive coach, I use Richard's *Mach II* in my coaching work. Richard is the best in the world at what he does, and I use his approach to help my clients become the best in the world at what they do."

— RACHEL CONERLY
Executive Coach, Collaborative Leaders, Inc.

"I work with the Franklin-Covey organization in their Personal Coaching Division. We handled the coaching for the Napoleon Hill Foundation, Tom Hopkins, Denis Waitley, Zig Ziglar, Brian Tracy and Stephen Covey. Richard's book quickly became a 'must read' item for our team. It has been a powerful tool in my personal life and I have watched it plant that all-important seed of hope and belief into other people's lives."

— DENNIS WALKER
Salt Lake City, UT

"I was extremely impressed with *Mach II*, particularly the way Richard Brooke defines success and vision. I even use excerpts of Richard's book in my success workshops."

— SHERRI DONAHUE
Motivational Speaker & Success Trainer

"Richard Brooke is that rarest phenomenon: a philosopher who spends as much time working as thinking. The result is a book that has been lived and is a life success guide that keeps it real. Real world, real time, real practical and powerful."

— CLIFTON H. JOLLEY, PHD
President, Advent Communications

"Admittedly Richard Brooke was no academic star. However he achieved massive financial success, breaking out of a dead-end job to live the luxurious lifestyle most only dream about. He shows the basis of his success: having a strong vision that will pull you through the hard times that inevitably occur in any occupation or opportunity. Produced in simple steps, *Mach II* gives an inspiring take on developing the mental attitude that will take you on to greater peaks of success."

— M.H. DENEKAMP
Amazon Book Review

"I have a copy of *Mach II* that I read once in a while when I need a funny, focused dose of the Law of Attraction. The LOA is everywhere, but this is one of the first works that speaks about it in other-than-secret terms."

— RICHARD LANOUE
Amazon Book Review Beaumont

"Richard Brooke has polished the art of motivating people who are unsatisfied with their lives. He condenses a life of work and teaching into a manual for CHANGE through embracing vision and motivation ... the most solid formula for achieving success in finding and becoming the person you want to be."

— Grady Harp
Rated as a Top 10 Reviewer, Amazon.com

"*Mach II* is a must-read for anyone in a Network Marketing business. It offers a very clear explanation of the Law of Attraction without the cloak and dagger of other popular books. I especially love his definition of vision. Read the book. It's worth every penny!"

— A. Cummings

"Richard Brooke is one of the finest men in the Network Marketing industry. He knows his stuff and produced *Mach II* with flying colors. I recommend this book and audio series to anyone who is committed to moving their business on the fast track."

— Peggy Long
Trainer, Coach & Author, *On This Rock*

"I have read *Mach II* over and over again. Prior to completing Richard Brooke's course work, I had no clue how to create a vision. Having a vision has now become a part of my being. I am amazed that what I write and live by actually does come true! Living by my vision has me knowing things will happen — versus hoping."

— Michelle Amiel
Delray Beach, FL

"I have become an evangelist for *Mach II*! It is a very informational read. I share this book with my business prospects so they will have a tool to transform their lives and reach whatever goals they choose."

— Mark Beaumier, Jr.
Painesville, OH

"If *Mach II* were the only book left in the world, we would survive and prosper! It is one of a kind."

— Ruby Cassidy
Charlotte, NC

"*Mach II* is terrific! Not only is it a 'must read' for the brand new Network Marketing distributor, it is destined to be the handbook for seasoned veterans of the industry."

— Tom Chenault
Host of *The Home-Based Business* radio show and daily prime time radio show, *Business for Breakfast*

"I just read *Mach II* and am moved. My entire team is getting Richard's book!"

— Jared Crebs

"It is truly amazing what we can create with our thoughts, focus and visualization. After reading *Mach II*, I can hardly wait to attend one of Richard's workshops!"

— Sheila Curtiss
Escondido, CA

"After reading *Mach II*, we created a 60-second script that we read every day, hoping it would help us achieve a new level with our company. Instead, we were awarded the most coveted award our company offers!"

— Dr. Norm Dawson
Corrales, NM

"My wife, who has never read any books on vision or mindset, read *Mach II* and it changed her life. The light came on! *Mach II* is so simple to understand; it's to the point, but still very complete."

— Tim Erickson
Nine Mile Falls, WA

"I ordered two of Richard Brooke's books: *The 4-Year Career* and *Mach II*. These books have changed my life and for that I am very grateful. They are two of the best books I have read yet on personal development and Network Marketing."

— Lenny Evans
Redlands, CA

"If you can only buy one book, *Mach II* is the book to buy!"

— Ray Gebauer
Mannatech, Presidential with an organization of 250,000

"*Mach II* awakened my dreams and inspire me. It is a must read to accompany any Network Marketing get-started program. Read this book, apply the material and you will succeed … it's that simple!"

— Jan Taylor
Henderson, Nevada

"I read *Mach II* three times, then gave it to my son to read for himself. It made me reflect on what I have accomplished and helped me refocus on my next accomplishment: clearing up the conflict in my thoughts. It took me a while to see my Vision, but I saw it and took the steps to acquire it. Now I live a great life and am working on a new Vision."

— Steve Jackson
Hamilton, Ontario

"I have four copies of *Mach II*; one for home, one for the car, and a couple to loan out. I have all of Richard Brooke's audio CDs as well. As the owner of a formidable personal development library, I can tell you that Richard's work is among my very favorite resources."

— Glenn Jaffas
Holland, MI

"Richard Brooke is well-known in my organization for many years. I bought hundreds of copies of *Mach II* in Russian translation, and this outstanding book has rendered enormous influence on the outlook of my downline."

— Roman Sobolevsky
Lvov, Ukraine

"Richard Brooke's *Mach II* is the most valuable gift I have ever received. His personal story and interesting analogies truly reach his readers!"

— Young Song
Korea

"Utilizing the concepts of *Mach II* has changed our lives! We have insight and an organized approach to achieve what is important to us and our future. It's a 'must read' for everyone seeking to secure a future of their own choosing."

— Don & Mary Lou Vollmer
Castle Pines, CO

"I read *Mach II* and definitely give it a 'thumbs up!' Richard Brooke does an excellent job of distilling the material into an easy to grasp, applicable format. I even had both of my teenage boys read it and purchased them for my organization to help them grasp a new vision."

— Jennifer Johnson
Coeur d'Alene, ID

"I am quite a success today and I owe a lot of my success to the teachings of Richard Brooke. I am doing fantastic and making more money than I ever thought I was capable of!"

— Ed Meyer
Midvale, ID

"I have to tell you, from page one, I could not put *Mach II* down; I read it cover to cover in one sitting. For anyone who owns a business, or oversees a staff, or is interested in self-improvement — for anyone, period — this book is a must have!"

— Nancy E. Nick
Post Falls, ID

"*Mach II* is a great book! I am giving a copy to all my new business builders. This is a book they must read!"

— Mary Jane Rothner
Salem, OR

"If you don't already have *Mach II*, get it! And get your hands on anything else Richard Brooke has ever produced, written or recorded. Doing so will be one of the greatest investments you could ever make!"

— Tony Michael
Dallas, TX

"I loved Richard's honesty when I heard him speak at the Mastermind event, and I love his book, *Mach II*!"

— Lasse Borg
Zinzino, Denmark

"I read *Mach II* on the plane ride home from a Mastermind event. Wow … thank you, Richard!"

— Melody Johnson

TABLE OF CONTENTS

FOREWORD

Maybe you are like I was, somewhere in between a little confused to completely in the dark about what I wanted to do with my life. And, if I did figure that out … how I was going to pull it off? I really wanted to be successful, to contribute, to be respected, to be secure, and to have financial freedom. But I didn't know how.

The normal rules for doing so didn't work for me: good grades, college, a family business or career counseling. Instead, I was fortunate to hook up with some people who had powerful alternatives, and I finally listened to them. The results have been staggering, at least to me.

I had to hear this information a lot of different ways before I heard it in a way that I "got it." I expect that when you study the flow of these secrets, you will get it, too. Then, all you have to do is hold on.

— Richard B. Brooke

• • • • •

This book is dedicated to
Kurt and Jeannie Robb
in honor of their gift of life.

▶ This is the true joy in life, being used for a purpose recognized by yourself as a mighty one. That is being a force of nature instead of a feverish, selfish little clod of ailments and grievances, complaining that the world will not devote itself to making you happy.

I am of the opinion that my life belongs to the whole community and as long as I live, it is my privilege to do for it whatever I can.

I want to be thoroughly used up when I die, for the harder I work, the more I live. I rejoice in life for its own sake. Life is no "brief candle" to me. It is a sort of splendid torch, which I have got hold of for the moment and I want to make it burn as brightly as possible before handing it on to future generations.

— George Bernard Shaw, 1856-1950
Quoted from the preface to the play,
Man and Superman (1907)

MY STORY

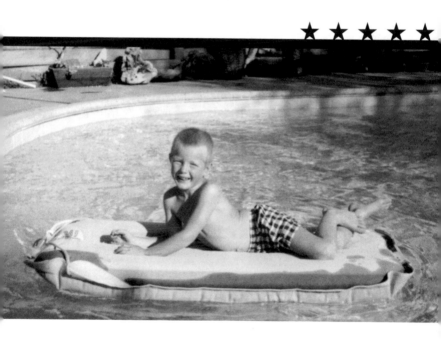

"The American Pioneers had to become successful entrepreneurs … the Indians would not hire them."

— Richard B. Brooke —

Richard and sister Debbie trail riding in Yosemite, California in 1961.

I grew up on a cattle ranch in Chowchilla, California. At the age of four, I stole a pair of sunglasses from Red's Market. When my mom asked me where I got them, I told her the *truth*. She made me take them back and apologize to Red. I was totally humiliated. I *decided* telling the truth was painful and not a smart thing to do.

In the fifth grade, a girl I liked sat with me at a movie. We held hands. The very next day, she "dumped me." I *decided* I wasn't good enough for the women I liked.

In the sixth grade, we moved from the ranch to the city. The cool guys (the ones all the girls liked) wore powder blue Levi cords. I was still wearing K-Mart jeans — the ones with the double-patched knees. I *decided* I was not cool.

My Core Beliefs About Me

- Telling The Truth Was Painful
- I Was Not Good Enough
- I Was Not Cool

In our developmental years we form our personality. These years encompass prenatal through about age five, and perhaps longer in children who are slow to develop emotionally. During these childhood years, without the vast background of context and reason we have as adults, we tend to experience events and "*decide*" *who we are versus deciding what happened*.

Just like millions of other kids my age, I formed a personality to cope with life as I perceived it. As a result of a few silly everyday circumstances, I created a belief system and a way of behaving to go along with my beliefs. It was hardly a winning personality; low self-esteem, driven to belong and be accepted — and, thanks to those sunglasses, I was a compulsive liar. I could have decided lots of different things about those early events. Why I decided what I did, I have no idea. The point is, my *creative childhood interpretations* of those circumstances became the truth for me — a truth that *could* have lasted for the rest of my life.

I was a typical negative thinker. Although my parents were affluent, college-educated ranchers in California, my downbeat attitude made success in life a long shot. My parents divorced when I was 17.

I hated school. I didn't study and skipped a lot of classes. I barely graduated with a D average, and so I didn't even try for college.

For a while I thought it might be nice to be a forest ranger. But then a ranger told me that I would need to get a college degree first. Even then, the ranger warned only 300 applicants were selected per year out of 3,000.

A nanosecond after he told me that, I decided that I couldn't be one of those 300. Of course, I was right. I couldn't, because I believed I couldn't.

Graduating high school (by cheating off Stan Callan's civics final), I started my professional career pumping gas at Pearson's Arco at the corner of G and Olive Streets in Merced, California. I also lived at the gas station — in my pickup camper with Chinook, my faithful dog. Eventually (after I failed to lock the front door of the gas station two nights in a row), my "ambition" led me to Foster Farms, the largest poultry processing plant in the world.

It was a union job that paid $3.05 an hour, complete with benefits, seniority, vacation, and best of all — retirement. I jumped at the opportunity. My job was to cut the chickens into parts as they flew past me on the production line … millions of chickens … billions of chickens. That's what I did for 450 to 530 minutes a day. Production people live their lives in minutes.

Although I was a hard worker, ambitious, and intelligent, there were some aspects of my personality that held me back. I disliked most other people. I refused to let anyone I considered less competent than myself ever tell me what to do. I worked my way up to teaching people how to cut up chickens. But, it didn't take long for my dynamic personality to put me back in my place. I told my boss, Wayne, that he should go to hell — and I said it in front of his boss, Mr. Hoyt. That's all it took to put me back on the production line.

Regardless, I loved the chicken plant and still love the people with whom I worked. At that time, I fully expected to spend the next thirty years of my life working there, building seniority (POWER), vacation time (FUN), and clicking off the years to retirement (FREEDOM). I thought I was really cutting it — life, not chickens.

That was 1977. I was 22.

▶ ON CHICKEN'S FRONT LINE

Walt Frazier has almost always been in "live hang." The term, like most things in a modern-day chicken slaughterhouse, is vivid and precise: chickens, fresh from the farm, are hung by their feet in metal shackles and carried off to the kill room. Ask most workers about live hang and they shake their heads ....

In a chicken plant, all tasks are calibrated to the second, and each worker, in effect, is a part of the machine. Frazier was a great live hanger and an efficient machine in his own right. He could grab a reluctant chicken off a conveyor belt and hoist it overhead at a pace of one bird every two seconds, real talent in a world defined almost exclusively by time and volume. Live hang's first shift runs from 5:48am to 2:18pm at this plant, and by shift's end, Frazier alone could feed about 10,000 birds into the Delmarva Peninsula's $1.6 billion-a-year chicken industry ....

Few places are more dangerous than a chicken plant: the U.S. Labor Department says one of every six poultry workers suffers work-related injury or illness every year. Crowding has even given rise to a special injury, "neighbor cuts," when workers inadvertently cut the person next to them.

Frazier, after two decades of what amounts to the front line of the chicken industry, can trace his career with his scars. Chicken claws have cut so deep and so often that his right forearm is a patchwork of curved lines. The black skin on his knuckles has been rubbed so raw that it has been discolored to permanent pink. Grabbing and lifting chickens has, over time, torn the lining of his wrists, resulting in two operations ....

Consumers want processed chicken — boneless and skinless, cut and molded — and technology has found no better alternative to the precision and efficiency of human hands. This places an extraordinary demand on the workers, the repetitive nature of cutting and moving chicken over time taxing hands, wrists, arms and shoulders.

The slaughterhouse challenges the senses. The plant smells like wet feathers. Temperatures range from below freezing — in what is known as the 28-degree-room, where packages await shipping — to 120 degrees by the scalder, which loosens feathers. In the summer, live hang becomes so unbearably hot that chickens can suffocate in less than a minute.

The din is such that yearly hearing tests are necessary. Water from high-pressure hoses soaks the concrete floor. Fat turns surfaces slick, blood drips from gutted chickens.

For Frazier, every day in live hang ended the same way. He removed his orange coveralls, streaked with dirt, feathers and chicken excrement. He took off his gloves, torn by countless claws. Off came the back brace. At home, in Bridgeville, Del., he soaked his hands in hot water, alcohol and salt, hands so sore it hurt to hold the telephone for long. "All the time, the numbness be there."

—Lena H. Sun & Gabriel Escobar

Excerpts from the article,
On Chicken's Front Line
(November, 1999)

The Rest of the Story

The rest of the story may sound like bragging … and I guess it is. However, I offer it with the greatest of humility.

My success since capturing the methods in this book has been significant compared to the $3.05-an-hour job I started with at the chicken plant. And yet, I am very clear that tens of thousands of other people around the world have accomplished billions more than I have, in every area of life. Mine is just an example for comparison: Chicken Chopper to C.E.O. to Multimillionaire.

If I can do it, you can do it.

I made my first million before the age of 30, advancing to the top sales-leader position in a marketing organization made up of more than 250,000 sales people. At age 31, I became that company's Executive Vice President.

At age 33, I accepted the opportunity to "turn around" a Network Marketing company. This company, when I joined it, was in a death spiral and technically bankrupt. It was almost $1 million in debt with no cash, no assets and no credit. With the help of a tremendous staff and my business partner, Randy Anderson, we turned this company into a role model for the Network Marketing industry.

In March 1992, at age 37, *SUCCESS* magazine featured

me and our company on its cover. This was the first time a mainstream business magazine featured Network Marketing in a positive light. At that time, this issue outsold every issue in *SUCCESS* magazine's almost 100-year history. *SUCCESS* called us "Millionaire Makers" and did a feature article on how the people we worked with and trained built "overnight empires." And they did — and still do. Not overnight, but many of our top sales leaders have built businesses worth well over $1 million. Several have become multimillionaires. *SUCCESS* magazine has featured our company three more times since then.

In 1993, Sterling & Stone Publishing asked me to co-author *The New Entrepreneurs: Business Visionaries for the 21st Century*.

In 1994, I was nominated *Inc.* magazine's Entrepreneur of the Year.

In 1996, *Working At Home* magazine co-featured me on their cover about how to get rich working from home.

In 1998, I was inducted into the Network Marketing Hall of Fame.

In 2002, I received the distinguished Distributor's Choice Award as one of the Top Five Trainers in Network Marketing.

Today, I continue to conduct personal and leadership development workshops and retreats, in addition to running a successful twenty-five-year-old Network Marketing company. Our company or products have been positively featured on NBC's *Dateline*, ABC's *20/20*, CBS's *Good Morning America*, *The Today Show*, *USA Today* (twice), the Academy Awards and Emmys, as well as in numerous mainstream and trade publications such as *Allure*, *Vogue*, *Health*, *New Beauty*, *InTouch*, *Men's Health*, *SUCCESS* and many more.

I've been to every state in our country at least twice, as well as 23 foreign countries. I've been the featured speaker for countless groups numbering in the hundreds, and several times, in the thousands. Although not every area of my life has been wonderful, my health is great, I love where I live and what I do, and I am blessed with dozens of loyal and loving friends and family.

I hope by now you're asking: "What happened?"

Here's what happened …

I changed. I changed my thoughts. I changed the people I paid attention to. I changed my mind. I changed my habits. I changed my attitude. I changed my clothes. I changed my opinions about me and about you. I changed what I read, what I watched on television, and what I listened to. I changed those deep-rooted decisions about who I was and who I would become.

It wasn't easy, but it was just as simple as the decisions I'd made early on. I just decided to be different and do different things and then I kept deciding those new decisions over and over and over again, until they caught hold. And then, all I did was hold on!

Change is possible for all of us. You may have heard lots of clichés about how we cannot change who we are … but just ask yourself: Have you changed? What events or insights in your life have changed what you believe and how you act? This is a good place to list them.

Think about people who have come and gone in your life; events — some joyous, some tragic. Think about wisdom you have gained. Have you changed? If you have, you can change even more. I suggest that if it is on purpose and by design, you and I can change more in the next year than we have our whole lives. And in the next ten years, we can become a wholly different person manifesting wholly different results.

Change is not only possible, it is inevitable. The only question is, who is going to design it? What has changed you?

1.

2.

3.

4.

5.

In May 1977, while still working in the chicken plant, I was introduced to a financial and personal development opportunity by one of my friends, Steve Spaulding, now deceased. The concept was called Network Marketing. Ironically, Steve was the guy who got me the job at the chicken plant. I think he introduced me to this new opportunity because he felt sorry for me.

There were several of our other buddies getting involved: Dave and Dan Austin, and the magnificent Jack Acker, now deceased. They were all friends who lived in the small ranching town of Merced, California. Although great guys, they were all seasonal workers at the local Ragu Spaghetti Sauce cannery, and — having mostly avoided any higher education at all — weren't the most credible bunch of fellows to follow into a financial opportunity. We were told that if we followed the company's plan, we could earn more than $60,000 per year — part time!

In 1977, the only people in the world who earned $60,000 per year were:

- Doctors or lawyers
- Well-educated professionals
- People given a successful business by their parents
- Those who inherited a lot of money
- Those lucky enough to have powerful connections in landing a super job

I knew this to be true.

I knew I wasn't any of those people, therefore …

I knew I would never earn $60,000 doing anything!

But boy did I ever want to earn $60,000, more than anything in the world! This posed a problem: *I wanted something I didn't expect would ever happen.* The leaders of this financial opportunity were prepared for me and my dilemma. Apparently, it was common. They conducted intense training courses designed to resolve the problem. Their star trainer was a man named Kurt Robb.

On August 3 and 4, 1977, we all — the guys and I and forty strangers — sat in the Ramada Inn in Bakersfield, California, and listened for hours as speaker after speaker jumped up and down, telling us that we really could earn $60,000 a year — no problem.

And then came Kurt Robb.

Kurt told us how he used to work for Ma Bell in an Oklahoma factory … that although he was content there, he wasn't achieving all he desired. And then, at the urging of his wife Jeannie, he quit and joined her in a Network Marketing venture ….

"Whether you think you can or you think you can't, you're right!"

— **Henry Ford** —

1863-1947, Founder, Ford Motor Company

He said he had the same problem we did — that he *wanted* something he *didn't believe* he could have. Jeannie believed he could achieve anything. But Kurt told us he didn't believe it. So, they struggled and struggled, trying anything they thought could break them out. Eventually, after applying what he was about to teach us, Kurt broke through his *self-imposed limitations* and became an extraordinary success. Kurt and Jeannie were now traveling the world, helping other people achieve their dreams, and having the time of their lives doing it.

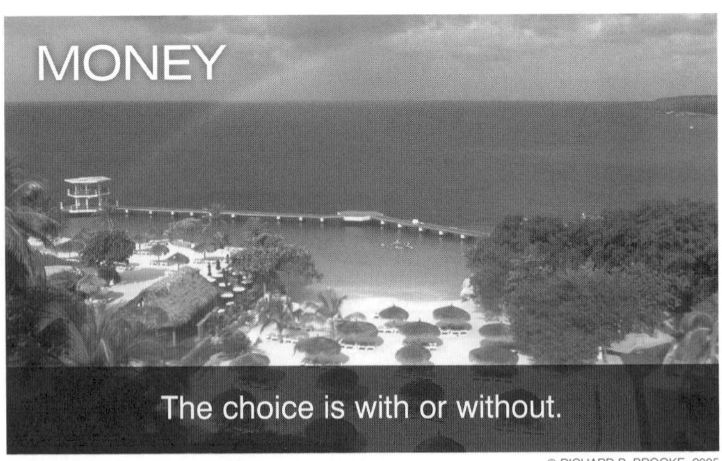
MONEY
The choice is with or without.

So we listened.

What we heard about was a system — a "specific, proven procedure," Kurt insisted — that would bring anyone anything they wanted. A simple system that had actually been used for thousands of years to support human beings in achieving their greatness.

As he laid out each step — what it was, how to use it and what result was sure to come — I saw something about succeeding that had never occurred to me before … that you and I can achieve just about ANYTHING we set out to achieve, and it has little or nothing to do with luck, education, money or connections. This was completely mind-blowing for me. It went against everything I knew to be true. So, I thought to myself: If this is true, why doesn't everyone know this? Why isn't this a required course throughout our school years?

How could algebra (whatever that is) be more important than this?

None of us ever went back to the cannery or the chicken plant. Every one of our lives changed that weekend.

Jack Acker passionately pursued his dreams with us for about five years, impacting everyone he touched with his gifts of laughter, fun, and a wicked golf game. We lost Jack to cancer.

Jim Acker, Dave Austin, Steve Spaulding, Bill Lane, Richard Brooke and John Callahan on their first cruise to the Bahamas.

Dan Austin used his experience as a stepping stone to a successful industrial film business – mostly filming brother Dave, who is a master in his trade today. Dave is consistently one of the highest paid Network Marketers in the world.

Before Steve Spaulding's passing, he was also a master in his trade. He was one of the best motivational speakers and trainers in the industry. Both Steve and Dave have contributed their gifts to tens of thousands of others; both are multimillionaires.

Something quite magical happened that day in Bakersfield. And I share these stories with you in the hope that you will open your mind to the possibilities these techniques offer you.

I received a great introduction to these ideas from Kurt Robb. Tragically, he died nine months after I met him. So I looked elsewhere for others who seemed to have insights into the idea of "success on purpose."

Over the last 30 years I have invested over $250,000 in course work of this nature — including many intensive coaching and workshop programs — to hone my understanding of "what makes me and others tick." I have read hundreds of books and listened over and over to hundreds of audio programs. Everything I have ever learned has come from the experiences and perspectives of other people on the same path.

The education I acquired and the scope of viewpoints has been broad, and much of it I would never use today. In the end, I came to see clearly certain distinctions that explained simply and powerfully how you and I function in "Action and Attraction." And I found a way to explain it that seemed to resonate with others looking to understand it.

Mach II is a version of how to explain and how to execute a set of truths that have been in play since the beginning of mankind. These truths have been taught for at least a hundred years. It is not new teaching, but rather a new way to see it for those continuing to seek clarity.

Mach II's focus is to draw out certain distinctions that I did not find in the other work I studied … distinctions that allowed me to see what was not entirely clear. The most insightful works that supported me were *Psycho-Cybernetics* by Dr. Maxwell Maltz, and the wide body of seminar work by Lou Tice of the Pacific Institute.

Here are the key distinctions you may get from studying *Mach II:*

1. You and I are infinite storehouses of creativity, physical energy, courage, enthusiasm and persistence. We can progressively accomplish anything we set our mind correctly towards. In fact, we have been our whole lives … whether we wanted to or not.

2. *Mach II* uses the word Vision to describe the "mindset," "expectation" or "belief." It is a potentially different version of the "Visionary" use, as *Mach II's* use of the word carries with it a very specific criteria for what constitutes a Vision. As Napoleon Hill wrote: "What the mind of man can conceive and believe, it can achieve." What *Mach II* does is focus on what that belief looks like and how to create it.

3. It is NOT desire that fuels our accomplishments. Desire points us in a direction, but desire alone is not useful beyond

pointing. Desire shows us what we really want. But it's a whole other story getting to where we need to go.

4. *Mach II* uniquely describes the "power to produce" as Motivation; and describes Motivation as the energies of Creativity, Enthusiasm, Persistence, Courage and Physical Energy. All of these together most certainly cause us to Act powerfully and Attract powerfully, as well. The combination of all of these energies "firing" at the same time creates a vibration that brings to us similar good fortune.

5. We are "motivated" to accomplish goals based on how technically correct our Visions are and how they contrast with what we currently are accomplishing. Nothing else really matters much … not how educated we are, how hard we work, how nice we are or how badly we want something. Creating the Motivation is all that really matters.

6. Visions are clearly distinct from Goals, and are vastly more powerful a tool in moving down a chosen success path.

7. A Vision is not really something to get, as we ALREADY have thousands of them and we are already motivated to bring them to fruition ... whether we want them to materialize or not. The trick is to change the Visions we have to ones that serve our Core Values, Gifts and Life Purpose.

I have focused all that I have learned into one pivotal concept and procedure called Vision and Self-Motivation.

If five guys from a small town can break out, so can you.

It's no fluke that a group of minimum wage, lower-than-low self-esteem, directionless, high school buddies found their magic and power and learned how to turn it up full blast. *Mach II With Your Hair On Fire* is about you making the same powerful discovery. Here's how ....

▶ At the pinnacle of his success, Kurt Robb was suddenly and tragically killed in the rugged surf of Hawaii. Jeannie was with him. It was their first success-spurred, "no expense spared" vacation.

Kurt's teachings had such a profound impact on my life that he instantly became one of the most important people in it. Then he left — for good.

While Kurt was alive and training me, I never implemented anything he taught me. I was "getting trained," "working on it," and "preparing." When I first heard of his death I reacted by quitting — feeling that without him always there to help me get ready, I couldn't go on. Hours after quitting, I realized that my reaction was a cowardly dishonoring of Kurt's gift, and that I could only honor his contribution by becoming, from that moment on, a source for others. No longer could I be "getting ready." I had to implement and teach others to do what he had taught me.

My life changed dramatically that day. That day, I decided to be the "Source" for myself and others, to do what I knew could be done.

—Richard B. Brooke

SUCCESS SECRET ONE:
SELF-MOTIVATION

"You miss 100 percent of the shots you never take."

— Wayne Gretzky —
Canadian Hockey Player; holds record for career goals scored.

Accelerating the Momentum

This book is about Motivation — Self-Motivation. It's about starring in, directing and producing the movie of your life — with powerful results. It's about taking your desires, hopes, dreams and aspirations and turning them into roaring fires of accomplishment. And, it is also about how to do this all by yourself … anywhere you want … anytime you choose … for the rest of your life!

However, this book is NOT about achieving everything you've ever wanted. That's not a place you will ever want to get to — not that you ever could. For along with having everything you want comes APATHY. This book is simply about accelerating the momentum of your every success for the rest of your life. People are happiest when they are in the process of achieving … when they're accomplishing something that's tremendously important to them. It's the anticipation of getting the intended result — knowing you're

So much of what the great athletes do to accomplish the impossible is done through visualization. Mach II captures exactly how it works; why it works; and how anyone can use it to do great things in their life.

— **John Elway** —
Super Bowl MVP & NFL Hall of Fame Quarterback

on the right track, moving forward, in momentum — that makes you happiest.

Do you remember when you bought your first car? Do you remember how you felt in the weeks, days and hours leading up to the purchase … the period of time when you knew you were going to get it, but you were still working on financing or delivery? Do you remember the high of anticipation? These feelings are the essence of my definition of success.

Do you remember the promise you made to yourself and others about how the car would never see rain; you would never eat in it or abuse it in any way?

Yes, and then what happened after you got the car? Do you remember how the feelings slowly diminished? If you were like me, it only took a couple of weeks before you were driving through mud, eating a burger and fries and yes, back in those days, puffing away on a cigarette. Achieving the result itself has such short-lived pleasure.

The essence of being truly alive comes with falling in love with the pursuit of your dreams … always stretching … always in momentum … always expecting the best.

This is Winning.

This is Success.

This is Living.

This is Happiness.

This is *Mach II With Your Hair On Fire.*

And Self-MOTIVATION is your key.

The Four Greatest Lies of Success

The following are what can be called "cultural paradigms," meaning they are the hidden rules of society. Sometimes they are in our face, placed there by our parents or other authority figures. Other times they are just the rules of the road; not so bold, but always there.

By referring to them as "lies," I am not suggesting that they are not valuable attributes or even often required for the achievement of specific goals. What I am suggesting is that these "rules" do not necessarily lead to success, as society would have us believe.

1. Desire Creates Success

Most people confuse Motivation with desire. We think because we want something badly enough we will have the energy to get it.

Yet, how many people do you know who have a strong desire for a great deal more in their lives?

And ... how many of them have had that desire for a long time?

How many are achieving it? The fact is, almost everyone desires health, wealth and happiness — and almost no one achieves all three. How many people do you know who even have two?

A Social Security study conducted by the Bureau of Labor Statistics revealed that of 100 people who started working at age 25, by the age of 65...

With forty years to plan and work for their future, only 5 percent — just five people — were financially successful!

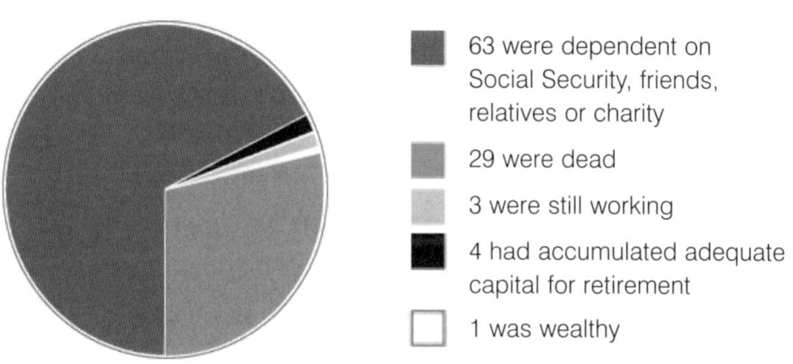
63 were dependent on Social Security, friends, relatives or charity
29 were dead
3 were still working
4 had accumulated adequate capital for retirement
1 was wealthy

Desire has absolutely NOTHING to do with Motivation.

Desire only creates the yearning for something, but not any of the actual magical energy it takes to stay on the path toward achieving it.

2. Hard Work Creates Success

Do you want to be successful? Then work hard! But haven't you *been* working hard? How many people do you know who have been working hard their whole life? If you worked twice as hard as you do now … if you worked twice as many hours every day … would you be successful? (Or would you be divorced or dead?) Does hard work necessarily have anything to do with success? I am not advocating not working hard. It just does not necessarily lead to you getting what you want. It is a great asset, but not the answer we have been led to believe it is.

3. Being a Good Person Creates Success

Be a good person. I am not advocating anything else. But what does being a good person have to do with success? How many successful jerks do you know? Haven't you seen the evidence that "money has no conscience?" It doesn't care where it goes. Neither does health, and in many domains of knowledge, neither does wisdom.

4. Getting a Good Education Will Lead to Your Success

Again, I am not advocating not getting as good an education as you can. Yet the world is filled with educated derelicts. Education does not insure anything. It confirms that we know how to study and pass tests. The age-old truth of getting great grades and getting into the best college is as good a strategy as working hard and being a good person. But it will not necessarily lead you to the good life.

THEN WHAT DOES LEAD ME TO GETTING WHAT I WANT IN LIFE?

The Secret to Success

If thousands of people have found the secret to success, then it's got to be Self-Motivation. They may not know it as Self-Motivation. Self-Motivation is that mysterious concoction of belief, confidence, positive expectations and creativity — a seeming abundance of physical, mental and emotional energy — that naturally propels us to our goals. Check it out for yourself.

If you could get yourself motivated enough …
And keep yourself motivated enough …
What do you think you could achieve?

Let's start out by defining Motivation:
Motivation is a powerful blend of physical, mental and emotional energies focused on creating an intended result.

It is the energy which LEADS us to ACT and causes us to ATTRACT.

Look at each of these separately and ask yourself:

If I could generate and sustain enough *Enthusiasm*, could I accomplish what I want?

THE KEY TO SUCCESS IS SELF-MOTIVATION

Enthusiasm
Courage
Persistence
Physical Energy
Creativity

Think about it. Think about what it feels like to be "on fire" about something you "intend" to do. Pick something you are now, or used to be, on fire about accomplishing. Remember how it felt? Do you remember how you thought about the goal? Allow that feeling to visit for a few seconds. Notice how your body chemistry changes … you can feel it. This is enthusiasm often dissected as: ENTHUS, meaning "God within;" and IASM for "I Am Sold Myself."

This one simple "energy" can fuel you to accomplish most anything all by itself.

ENTHUSIASM
Your God within. I am sold myself.
© RICHARD B. BROOKE, 2005

Take anything you might like to accomplish now and ask yourself: If you could get yourself — and keep yourself — enthusiastic enough about the process required, what could you accomplish? Think about the daily "must dos" that a lack of enthusiasm can keep you from doing, and for which an abundance of enthusiasm make it naturally easy.

Think about the workouts, the meal choices, the prospecting, the studying or practice required to achieve the goal. What could you accomplish if those daily or weekly "must dos" were naturally effortless?

If I could get and keep enough *Courage,* could I?

Think about courage. Courage is not a genetic quality. Courage is a state of mind and heart. Courageous people see the same danger as others do. They just act anyway. They "make up" something different about their ability to be successful.

Courage shows up hugely in the "must dos" of prospecting, whether you are in real estate, mortgage sales, fund raising or Network Marketing. If you can prospect effortlessly, fluidly, naturally and powerfully, then you know you will be as successful as you choose to be.

But what do we do when we think of a prospect and courage is in short supply?

Right, we "chicken out" by making up something about the

COURAGE
Seeing the danger and acting anyway.

Right, we "chicken out" by making up something about the outcome that sends us packing. Our path to success is full of Ys in the road. One path leads to success, the other to frustration. At each Y in the road we get to be a Chicken or a Champion. Courage is essential for Champions.

If I could get and keep enough *Persistence,* could I?

By now you have probably caught on to how Motivation makes all the difference in the world and how Persistence is absolutely essential, as well.

Every worthwhile venture will be riddled with setbacks. Not everyone on our path will share our Vision. Some will have opposing Visions. We will get knocked down … sometimes so hard it takes everything we have to just see the possibility of getting up again. Motivated people not only see getting up again, they bounce off the mat. They have to get up again.

So think about not only your life, but others you know. Who do you know that could have enjoyed enormous success had they just been able to pull themselves up off the mat one more time? When have you quit short of success? Perhaps you will never know what you missed. Perhaps you can see the power of persistence now.

And persistence, like enthusiasm and courage, are NOT genetic. They are the forces of Motivation and they can be created to flow on demand, on purpose for any project anytime you want.

If I could get and keep enough *Physical Energy,* could I?

Physical Energy. Probably everything we set out to do requires it. Some Visions, like finishing the Ironman competition, require trainloads of it. The Ironman requires a 2.4-mile swim, 112-mile bike ride followed by 26.2-mile run. Hundreds of people, many who are first-timers, do this every June in my hometown of Coeur d'Alene, Idaho, sometimes in 60-degree water and 90-degree heat. I know people in their sixties who have done it for the first time.

Can you imagine competing in that race? Can you imagine how much more physical energy you would need than you have now? Can you imagine the training regimen of two to four hours every day for four to twelve months?

Iron men and women summon the physical energy to pull it off, and it is not genetic. It is pure Motivation.

If I could get and keep enough *Creativity,* could I?

And finally, there is creativity. There are two distinct forms of creativity as it applies to Motivation.

The first is problem solving. You and I solve problems by

putting our brains to work on solutions. Our innate creativity looks for ways to solve problems, which is sometimes adding 2 plus 2 to equal 5, and sometimes just finding a new perspective or a new way of saying something that moves us forward.

One way of looking at achieving any goal is to say that the only thing standing between where we are now and where we want to be is a series of problems. Solve the problems and you progressively achieve more of the goal.

Creativity solves problems. Creativity is not genetic. Even the most brilliant people in history are, or were, only marginally smarter than any of us. And the most brilliant are often vastly more motivated by vastly clearer and more powerful Visions.

The second form of creativity is what I like to call Red Lights and Green Lights, or "creative interpretations." We have the creativity to "see" things in a certain light or with certain color glasses. This is when we see things in the light of "I can do it" or "it will work out" or "they will enjoy what I have to offer" or "this will be fun" or "this will be easy."

When we see things this way, we get a Green Light and nothing will stop us from acting on it.

When we "make up" an outcome that does not look easy or fun or successful, we get a Red Light and we find a creative excuse for why now is not a good time to act.

An example worth millions in itself is in prospecting for new clients or associates. When a motivated person "sees" a prospect, they naturally "make up" that approaching them is a good thing and it will work out for both parties. "Seeing" it that way leads them to make a comfortable, easy, fun and most importantly, a confident approach and make it right away. The results will always be better than a scared, timid, forced approach or obviously no approach at all.

How many giant prospects have you "creatively" avoided over the years? How much momentum and progress do you think it may have cost you?

What if you could get yourself and keep yourself "turning on the Green Lights" on your path? What could you accomplish? How fast could you get it done?

CREATIVITY
Making up ... I can do. I will do. I am doing!

Creativity is not the exclusive property of genius. Creative thought is the direct result of being MOTIVATED.

We all have the ability to generate creative thoughts whenever and wherever we want.

The same is true for physical energy, courage, enthusiasm and persistence. These energies and decision-making abilities are available to us on demand, in extraordinary quantities. Our emotional state of mind determines when and how we unleash them.

▶ OF ELEPHANTS AND FLEAS

Have you ever wondered how the circus keeps a 4,500-pound elephant tied up with only a flimsy, little rope around one of its huge ankles?

Simple conditioning.

When the elephant is a little baby (weighing only a couple hundred pounds), they secure one of its hind legs with a heavy steel chain. Every time the elephant tries to wander off, the chain jerks the animal back. After a while the elephant's ankle gets raw and sore. If it continues to tug at the chain, it experiences more and more pain.

It doesn't take too long with this kind of conditioning for the elephant to decide that tugging equals pain.

Eventually, a simple strand of rope is all it takes to restrain the huge creature.

Fleas — as the positive mental attitude guru Zig Ziglar has taught us — are trained in a similar fashion. The trainers put their fleas in glass jars and secure them with a cover on top. As the fleas try to jump out of the jar, they continuously bang their heads on the lid.

The flea trainer knows when his job is done because the fleas — expecting to be stopped by the lid — will jump no higher than the cap of the jar regardless of how much they want out. Then the lid can come off. The fleas have decided that jumping high is painful.

You and I are a lot like fleas [and elephants].

—Hanzo K.T. Nq
Excerpt from the article,
Change for the Better and Good

REVIEWING THE SCRIPT

THE ONE THAT'S ALREADY IN PLACE

"Restlessness is discontent, and discontent is the first necessity of progress."

— THOMAS A. EDISON —
1847-1931, American Inventor

Whether You Know It Or Not …
Whether You Want It To Or Not …

Your heart beats 103,680 times a day.

You breathe 23,040 times a day.

You generate 3,000,000 nervous impulses a second.

Your stomach develops an acid strong enough to dissolve nails.

Your entire body runs on very small, electrically charged particles.

And all of this is happening whether you know it or not … whether you want it to or not … and,

You already have Visions that motivate you to do what you are already doing.

TIME
Wasting it is easy until you do not have any left.

One of the primary unconscious functions of the human mind is releasing, on demand, sufficient levels of Self-Motivation. Your mind, through your Vision, creates and produces enthusiasm, courage, persistence and, most importantly, creativity. This is a natural, ongoing process. You are either aware of this gargantuan power and manage it to produce your intended results, or you allow it to run rampant — amuck and aimless — usually at little more than idle speed, chasing its tail in a vicious cycle of mediocrity. Don't ask me why about all of that; I'm in total wonderment. But the fact is, your mind does produce this effect for you. Your script is already in place — it's even self-monitoring.

The following statement communicates this as best I can:

> **To the degree that there is a contrast between what we have decided should be happening (Visions) and what is happening (current results), MOTIVATION naturally, effortlessly, powerfully and infinitely flows.**

It does this instantly, as soon as it recognizes that a contrast exists.

The best analogy for how this works is a thermostat.

Let's say the actual temperature (what *is* happening or your current results) is 65 degrees, and you set the thermostat at 70 degrees (what you've decided *should* be happening or your goal). There is a contrast between them. So, the thermostat signals the heater to produce heat (Motivation) until the temperature hits 70 degrees; at which time the thermostat signals the heater to stop. The temperature in the room starts to cool back down almost immediately.

When it drops below 70 degrees, Motivation (in the form of heat) begins to flow and the warming-up process begins again. Back and forth, back and forth, the temperature rises and falls, constantly in search of 70 degrees. *(Thank you, Bob Proctor: www.BobProctor.com.)*

Our Vision: The Thermostat

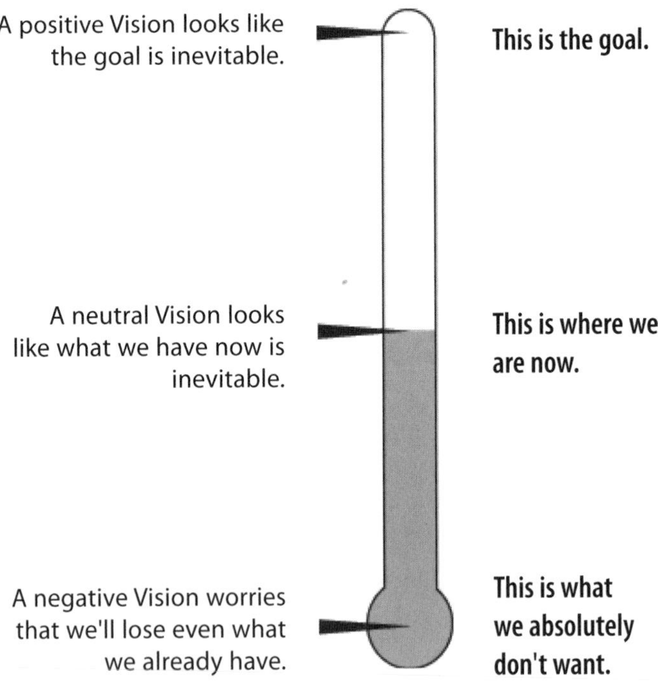
A positive Vision looks like the goal is inevitable.
This is the goal.
A neutral Vision looks like what we have now is inevitable.
This is where we are now.
A negative Vision worries that we'll lose even what we already have.
This is what we absolutely don't want.

So, when what is happening in your life contrasts with what you decide *should* be happening, the "thermostat" in your mind releases Motivation to bring the two together to create alignment. As the two come together, Motivation is momentarily reduced, only firing up again as they drift apart.

If there is no difference between what *is* going on and what you *expect* to be going on, you have no Motivation.

- There is nothing for your mind to pursue.
- You have no need for physical energy, enthusiasm, courage, persistence or creativity.
- You are, in a word, apathetic.
- Some people call it lazy, others bored.
- Lost souls in the sea of humanity.
- Victims of their own mind crimes.

Lemmings leading themselves off the cliffs of resignation, despair … hopelessness.

Your mind doesn't care about what you want — or what you're willing to work hard for. It only cares that you perform in accordance with what you expect for yourself. If that requires an adjustment up or down, one step forward or two steps back, your mind doesn't care. It's like a script that is already in place.

There are Three Basic Forms of Vision: On Fire, Apathetic, or Self-Destructive

On Fire

A **positive** Vision is aligned with your goals and will motivate you to achieve those goals.

Apathetic

A **neutral** Vision will create apathy or only enough Motivation to sustain the status quo. This Vision is not aligned with your goals, but rather reflects your current results.

Self Destructive

A **negative** Vision (worry) will actually motivate you to sabotage all current results. This Vision is not aligned with your goals or your current results, but rather is even further away from where you want to be.

On Fire

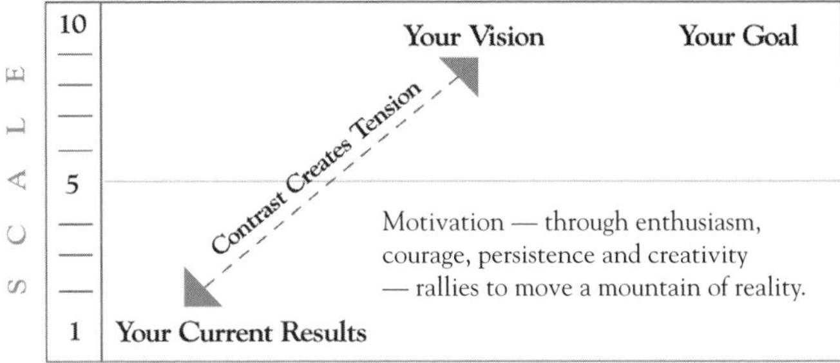

Apathetic

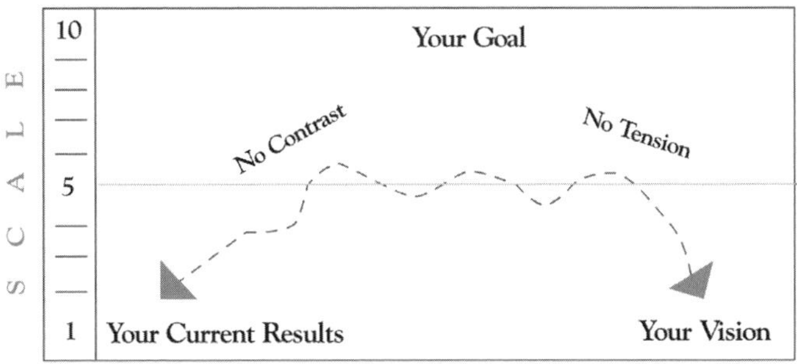

Self-Destructive

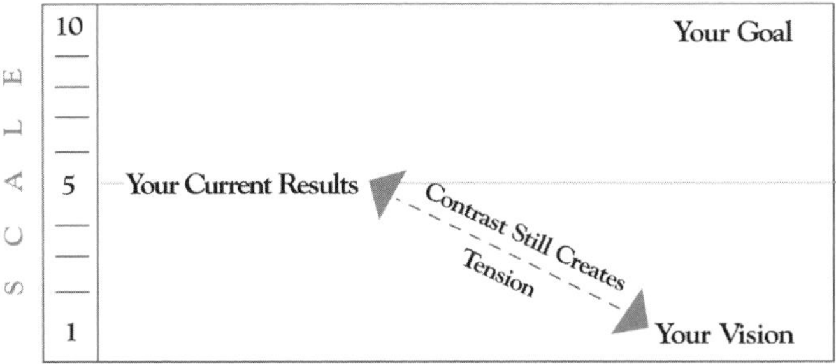

In her article titled, *Expectations May Alter Outcomes Far More Than We Realize* (*Wall Street Journal*, Science Journal; November 7, 2003), Sharon Begley put it this way:

"The power of expectations in the classroom is downright scary. In a typical experiment, elementary school teachers were told that one group of kids had done extraordinarily well on a test that predicts intellectual 'blooming,' and so would make remarkable academic gains. The test seemed prescient: After a few months, the 'bloomers' it identified had achieved statistically significant gains over the other students.

"In reality, there was no such test. To the contrary: The kids the teachers thought were bloomers included students from every ability level ... The only difference was in the mind and expectations of the teacher, yet those expectations produced clear academic differences."

Why Diets (and other things) Don't Work ...

Motivation is not the only force that can lead you to action. It is the only thing that can sustain you. Sometimes your reality can be altered by force, or by the impact the Motivation of other people has on you.

For example, what happens if, through hard work, desire, circumstances, or just plain luck, you create a result that differs significantly from what you normally would expect?

Let's say you've had a particularly good month in business and you earned twice as much money as you normally make. Or, perhaps you developed this burning desire to get back in shape physically, so you watched what you ate and worked out consistently for a whole month. You lost weight and looked great.

But then what happens?

You gain back the weight you lost — and then some!

Why?

Unless you quickly change your decision about you, your mind will unleash whatever subtle, yet powerful motivation is needed to bring you right back in line with what you really thought would happen — even if those thoughts are not what you want.

In this example, although you did lose the weight and looked great, you were still expecting to be overweight. Sooner or later, you were destined to be back where you started — out of shape and overweight — simply because that's what you were motivated to do. Remember, this is all natural and automatic. It's instinctive. It does not matter what you want and work hard for. You get what you expect. In sports when this happens, it's called choking.

Here is how this system played out in my money-making efforts. When I started out in my new $60,000-a-year

Network Marketing opportunity, I started with a decision that I could not make that kind of money. I *wanted* to make it. I *hoped* I could make it. I *wished* somehow I would get lucky. And, I didn't want anyone to know that I didn't think I could do it, so I *tried*.

I worked really hard; I invested everything I could get my hands on. I traveled everywhere, learned everything I could, and I made $12,000 my first year. Then I made another $12,000 my second year. (This is the same income I earned as a chicken cutter.)

Then I got tired of working so hard, so I took it a little easier and earned $4,000 my third year. You see, even though I wanted to earn $60,000 and I did everything I could think of to do it, I was working against an anchor dropped years earlier. A life-limiting decision like, "I wasn't good enough." (Remember the girl who dumped me in the fifth grade?) "I didn't need anybody." A bad position to be in when you're supposedly building a network of thousands.

So finally, after losing everything I had, including my home, three cars (repossessed), and all my credit, I finally hit bottom and I woke up. You see, even though I had been taught what to do to succeed, "I didn't need anybody," including some of the greatest minds of our time. I "tried" to make myself succeed. I tried to force it without changing what I thought about me. In my desperation (faced with returning to the chicken plant a failure), I decided to implement what Kurt Robb had taught me three years earlier.

I went to work on my head — my thoughts — what I held to be true, literally changing my mind about what I had decided about me. It worked. Within six months, I was earning $10,000 per month — within two years I was earning almost $40,000 per month. Think about that: $4,000 a year to $400,000 within two years!

Everything changed for me when I developed the willingness to train myself to think like a successful person.

Of course, most people lack the success thought process, initially. But I had an even worse problem. I lacked the willingness to acquire the success thought process. And that will stop anyone dead in their tracks.

The first time I was confronted with the science of Motivation, I rebelled. In training sessions, my instructor urged me to write down my goals and to study motivational books like *Think and Grow Rich*, by Napoleon Hill.

"If you read this book," the instructor promised, "and read other books like it and listen to tapes by successful people, you will begin to think the way they do.

And, once you start thinking those thoughts and believing those beliefs, you will become as successful as they are."

I thought it was baloney. My problem was that I "knew" that success had nothing to do with my thought process. Success came from getting straight As in college and having a Rolodex filled with influential connections. Everyone knew that. But, I read the book anyway.

At first, I hated *Think and Grow Rich.* It might as well have been written in Greek. I took over a year to slog through the slender volume, which many readers devour in a matter of days. The thoughts in this book were so contrary to my beliefs, I rejected them. That book and I were like repelling magnets, like water off a duck's back.

If only I knew what I was rejecting!

In the early years of this century, the legendary steel mogul Andrew Carnegie had imparted to Napoleon Hill — at the time, a struggling young journalist — what Carnegie believed to be the secret of his success. Hill then spent the next 20 years interviewing over 500 other wealthy and successful men, including Theodore Roosevelt and Thomas Edison, in order to gain their secrets. The results of his epic survey were revealed in Hill's classic books, *The Law of Success* (1928) and *Think and Grow Rich* (1937). Hill had discovered that all great achievers build their success around a single, simple principle, which alone had the power to transform a pauper into a billionaire. But, I didn't want to hear it. I thought I knew better.

I might have gone through my whole life rejecting this life-giving information. But, as so often happens, I was saved by a personal crisis. Few things are more conducive to action than having your back to the wall. I found that out the hard way. My greatest despair led to my ultimate salvation.

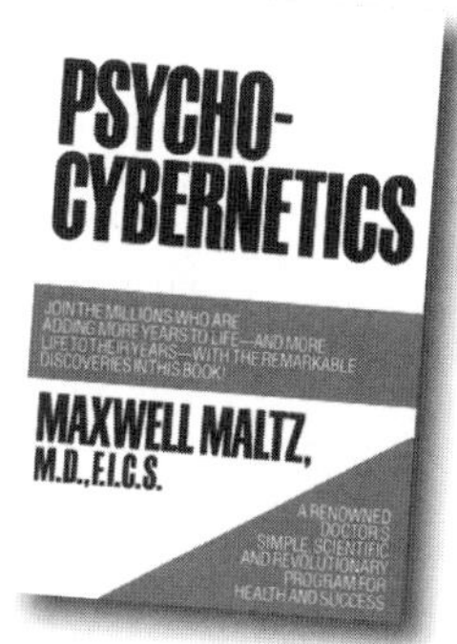

I set to work mapping out my goals — something Robb had told me to do years before. I started every day with a chapter of Napoleon Hill or a bracing dose of some other motivational book or tape. I read *As a Man Thinketh* by James Allen, *Psycho-Cybernetics* by Dr. Maxwell Maltz, Og Mandino's *The Greatest Secret in the World*, *The Magic in Believing* by Claude M. Bristol and many more. All day long, I would repeat positive phrases to myself, programming my subconscious mind to expect success. At night, I closed my eyes and visualized myself closing sales, recruiting top performers into my downline, and raking in scads of cold, hard cash.

At times, I felt like an idiot. Was this really me? The perennial skeptic? The cynic? Was I really behaving like all those wacky "positive thinkers" I'd mocked and teased for so many years?

Yes I was. And in no time at all, my new regimen began to bear fruit — big fruit. I expressed my new philosophy by quoting Napoleon Hill:

> **"The world has the habit of making room for the man whose words and actions show that he knows where he is going."**

I had learned the secret to success — that single, simple principle about which Napoleon Hill had written more than 50 years before. It was the power of goal setting.

Most people have goal setting confused with desire. People think that if you write down all the things that you desire, that's goal setting. It's not. Everyone is a goal setter and a goal achiever, whether consciously or not. Goal setting only works when your goal becomes your MINDSET or EXPECTATION. If all you do is think of things you want and write them down, your "wanter" will be working really well, but your "getter" will still be asleep. Goals have to become beliefs and expectations. You have to believe what you want is actually inevitable.

In the early days, I expected to fail. That was my unconscious goal, and I "achieved" it again and again, much to my dismay.

When I tried to recruit someone into my downline, I'd say something like, "Gee, I don't know if you'd be interested, but maybe you'd like to hear about this part-time opportunity …."

Deep down inside, I didn't really believe that anybody in his right mind would sign up for my downline — and it showed. My recruits were few and far between. Most failed to excel and dropped out after a short time. Try as I might, I could never manage to land the "Big Fish" — that top-level sales performer who would catapult his lucky sponsor (me) to overnight riches.

But as I began to take charge of my own daily thought process, to interrupt my negative thoughts as they appeared and to consciously evict them from my mind, something happened. My beliefs began to change. I began to expect success. I felt more powerful even though I was not producing any better results. I felt more at peace and safe. I felt optimistic. I was having a little more fun. I was managing what I was thinking, and what I was thinking was changing how I felt … both about me and how I felt about others.

Then I met Jerry Schaub.

Jerry was just another prospect who agreed to hear my presentation. Just like hundreds before. But I felt different, both to me and to this prospect … just enough different for him to see the opportunity and feel it all the way to his bones.

I went through the same sales presentation routine that I always did. But he looked down at my yellow pad of scribbles and said, "I can do this. Just show me how." And he meant it! Jerry Schaub was a tiger. Over the next year, he recruited hundreds of people into my downline. I earned $100,000 in commissions from Jerry's sales in that one year alone. My confidence soared and I went out and found myself three or four more Jerry Schaubs in the next year.

I became a master recruiter. I wasn't using any new technique. I was selling the same opportunity I'd been selling for four years. The only thing different was my willingness to train myself to think like a successful person. Before I began to change the way I thought, I was simply projecting too much doubt. People would sense something was wrong, and then put me off. But now, my energy level matched the words I was saying. People pay much more attention to who you are than to what you're saying.

These ideas have been around for centuries. All you have to do is use them.

LEADERSHIP
Parting the seas with your Vision
so that others may venture out.

VISIONS

"We hope vaguely, but dread precisely."

— Paul Valéry —

1871-1945, French Poet, Essayist & Critic

How You See Yourself

How you see yourself is through a series of pictures, like scenes from a movie, which you visualize in your mind's eye. This movie contains vivid scenes of your expectations, of how you imagine you will perform, or of what will happen in any given situation or set of circumstances. And, you have a unique and different set of pictures for each and every conceivable situation you might encounter in your life. They are all based on the decisions you have made about you.

THESE ARE YOUR VISIONS.

Do the following exercise to see for yourself:

Take something that you want — anything that's important to you and that you truly desire. Close your eyes and visualize yourself in possession of this; already having it … already doing it … already being it. "Tune in" the movie of you in that specific situation.

Let yourself flow with it. Watch the movie. Let yourself FEEL how it would feel. LISTEN to the voices, yours and others. Hear the sound-track of your life at that moment. Do that right now. Take one minute. Stop. Check your watch … give yourself 60 seconds.

This exercise can be one of the most important moments in

this book. Don't cheat yourself like I did. Do the work. Don't turn the page until you do the work. Close your eyes. In one minute, open them and answer the following questions:

1. On a scale of 1 to 10, was the picture you saw clear? (1 being a blank or snowy screen, and 10 a crystal-clear, wide-screen, high-definition, Dolby surround-sound movie Vision.)

   (Unclear) 1 2 3 4 5 6 7 8 9 10 (Clear)

2. On a scale of 1 to 10, did you feel a sense of positive or negative expectation regarding whether that result would (not could) actually happen or not?

   (Negative) 1 2 3 4 5 6 7 8 9 10 (Positive)

3. On a scale of 1 to 10, did you feel you really deserved it?

   (No) 1 2 3 4 5 6 7 8 9 10 (Yes)

Total up your points!

24-30: There is a high probability that you are on your way. HANG ON!

20-24: Something is standing in between you and what you want. You will want to do some aggressive Vision work to free this up. And, you may be making some progress.

16-20: You may want this, but you really only expect for things to stay the same as they are now. You must reinvent your beliefs about this goal.

Below 16: Not only do you not believe this will happen, exactly the opposite could happen. Worry is a Vision, too. And, you can replace worry with a Vision of success.

The decisions you have made about yourself create the picture you held in your mind throughout the last exercise. Your decisions are created by input you've received, which comes to you as conversations or experiences. This conversation originates from one or all of the following:

Outside input — such as what people have told you.

Experiences you've had — "the facts."

Your internal dialogue — your own conscious mind chatter.

The input you receive is just like programming a computer. Without software — the input — a computer is useless. So, in a very real sense, we ARE our programming — our movie script.

Our minds are the most intricate, powerful computers imaginable. They're literally worth billions in what they can enable us to accomplish. Just ask Bill Gates. (His net worth at the time of this reprinting is more than $56 billion, give or take a couple.) This self-made billionaire has not only created a fortune producing powerful software products, it's his own mental software programs that are worth billions of dollars.

The problem with our "computer" is that we've let just about everyone we've ever met program it!

Worse yet, we let *ourselves* program it. And, we usually don't know the first thing about how to write functional programs — much less the elegant ones that create the Motivation to lead us to break through our barriers to success.

Let's look at the three kinds of software we've been using to program ourselves.

Other People's Input

Whether from our parents, relatives, friends, teachers, television, the clergy, music, books, newspapers, movies, magazines, etc., one major source of our beliefs of what's expected of us was formed by input from outside influences. And, the more respected and admired the source, the more quickly we adopted that input as "true" and believed it unquestionably.

Here are some examples of other people's input:

NEGATIVE

- Don't put all your eggs in one basket.
- You're not good enough.
- Why can't you be like ______?
- You can't do that.
- What are you … nuts?
- The economy is headed for trouble.

- It's dangerous out there. Be careful.
- Why do you keep screwing up?
- Just keep your nose to the grind stone.
- Don't get your hopes up.
- What makes you think you can do that?

POSITIVE

- We love you no matter what.
- You can do anything you set your heart and mind to.
- You are the smartest.
- You deserve nothing but the best.
- We are with you all the way.
- We are always here for you.
- Dream big. Life is worth it.
- Live life to its fullest.
- You are so beautiful.
- Everyone loves and admires you.

▶ THINK YOURSELF STRONG

You may not need to actually go to the gym to get the benefits of a gym workout. Just imagining yourself there may do the job. Dave Smith, a sports psychology researcher at Manchester Metropolitan University in England, gathered 18 men and had six of them contract their pinkie fingers as hard as they could for 20 minutes a day, two times a week. Six others were instructed to just imagine

Experience

A second powerful source of beliefs comes from your past experiences. These are real, live testimonials — proof positive of who you are and what you are actually capable of doing. How can you argue these "facts" with such compelling evidence? There is a way to use only good and replace the bad. Check out these examples:

NEGATIVE

- You've always had a weight problem.
- You've never earned more than $___ in your life.
- You have problems with relationships.
- Every time you've tried something new, you've failed.

POSITIVE

- You have succeeded at other things that were new for you.
- You have increased your income at times before.

themselves doing the exercises. And a third control group of six did nothing at all. After 30 days, the pinkies of the first group were 33 percent stronger. Those of the control group were unchanged. But the men who had visualized themselves doing the pinkie crunches actually increased their strength by 16 percent.

— *Natural Health*, March 1999

- You have faced fear before and done it anyway.
- You have learned new things and excelled at them.
- You can change. You have before.

Self-Talk

The third — and potentially the most powerful influence in the creation of your beliefs — comes from the *thoughts and feelings* you tell yourself about your own experiences, and what you've told yourself about the input you received from other people.

For example, you recently read an article about how bad the economy in your area is and what a bleak future lay ahead for local businesses. The input you received was limited to the above subject, and you read it only once. But what did you

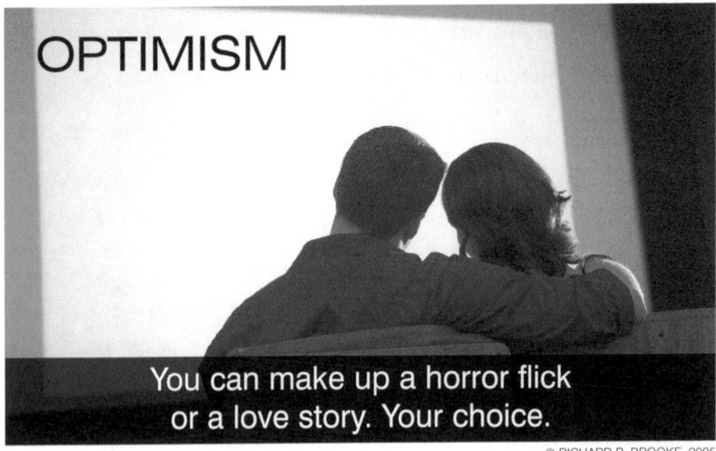
OPTIMISM
You can make up a horror flick
or a love story. Your choice.

add to it as you talked with yourself about what you thought and felt about what you had read?

Did you give it any additional credibility? After all, it appeared in a respected publication, and they — whoever they are — must know more about it than you do. Did you make the gloomy economic picture all the more vivid by imagining other negative "what if" scenarios, while combining what you'd read with your own fantasies and fears?

How often did you take that original story and clarify the details, add to it, expand and enhance it in your mind, giving it greater weight, more richness and additional credibility? And, how many times did you have these conversations with yourself? Once? Three or four more times? Dozens? Hundreds? Thousands? Look to see if all that you added — and the number of times you reviewed it — did not far outweigh the true impact of that single original piece of outside input.

Another example: Can you remember a single experience you've had that's similar to the following one, which happened to me?

One time, when I was playing little league, I got hit by a pitch. It was probably a 40-mile-per-hour "slow ball," but boy, it really hurt! And I cried. And I was humiliated because my buddies saw me cry. The incident happened only once. It happened when I was in the fifth grade, but I've thought about it and relived it at least a thousand times — especially when I'm playing baseball — which oddly enough, is about as often now as when I jump out of burning buildings.

In a nuts-o kind of way, baseball scares the heck out of me now. I'm afraid of being hit by a pitch. Not because I was hit by one single pitch, once way back in fifth grade, but because I've been hit and hurt and I've cried and have been humiliated thousands of times! Do the same thing over and over a thousand times and it makes quite an impression on what you expect will happen the next time. I can't even sit on the couch and watch a ball game on television without being hit by a pitch! Now, if I wanted to pursue a career or even the hobby of baseball I would need to replace the "Hit with the Pitch" movie in my mind with one of me winning the World Series. And I would need to watch it a thousand times.

The reason our "rerun" conversations and self-talk have such a powerful effect is due to one of the most profound statements we can make about the human mind. It's truly the most useful gift given to mankind:

To the degree there is *clarity,* the mind does not distinguish between an actual experience and one that has been vividly imagined!

Prove it to yourself.

Have you ever cried at a movie?

Have you ever screamed at a movie?

Have you ever laughed at a movie?

All of these moments are vividly imagined events that you — your body, your mind and your soul — reacted to as though they were real.

▶ GOALS VERSUS VISIONS

The more people read about Vision and the Motivation it produces, the more their traditional training about goals seems at odds with it. Let me assure you it is not. Goals are a very valuable technology for "focusing the mind" (Vision). Written goals have been documented to be 10 to 100 times more effective than "thinking you are thinking" about them.

Goals rely on several things that Visions do not rely upon.

Goals rely on deadlines. Deadlines can be very valuable. They create a sense of urgency, reducing procrastination. People who get committed to the deadlines within their goals — and are empowered by those deadlines — find they can produce more in a few days than the same person would normally produce in a few months.

Some people may be disempowered by deadlines. The looming date creates self-talk like: "I can't hit this deadline." In these cases, deadlines are not powerful.

Goals also rely on strategies or plans. Plans are important and anyone can tell you that the plan you start with is not usually the plan with which you end. Plans change ... sometimes overnight.

If you have a short-term goal and you feel like a deadline empowers you, by all means write out the goal and include the deadline. However, this is not a Vision. Often deadlines are there whether we want them or not, as in contests or end-of-the-business-month cycles. Longer term goals are not well served with deadlines, as without the deadline you may have achieved it earlier. If you do write out a goal for a short-term deadline objective, also write out a Vision of you already in possession of it or having achieved it.

Use both tools (goals and Visions) to get you there.

One of the challenges with deadlines is they are, in themselves, an affirmation that you do not currently own or possess what it is you want. You are affirming you will get it, which affirms you do not have it. The mind does not respond well to what you say you want, or even to what you say you will get. It responds to what you say is so NOW, and how that NOW contrasts with what you have. The contrast produces Motivation to close the gap.

Plans are valuable and a motivated person will create and keep creating a plan until it works. A motivated person does not worry about the "how," as they know the how will come. Creativity (Motivation) will create the how.

Create the Motivation and everything else you need — money, people, plans, ideas — will either be created by you, or it will be attracted to you.

Goal setting is an effective tool due to the way the mind captures and processes the goal. However, the way the goal is phrased versus the way a Vision is phrased makes goals vastly less effective for inspiring what it takes (Motivation) to get it done. Always use a Vision and if deadlines empower you, use them for short-term objectives.

YOUR MOVIE IS REAL

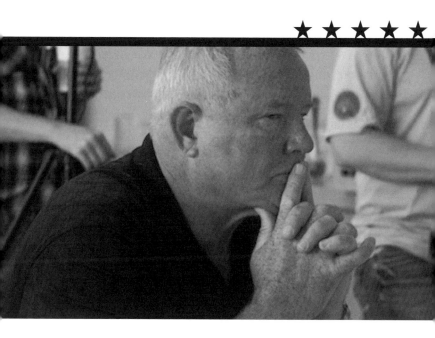

"The truth that makes men free is, for the most part, the truth which men prefer not to hear."

— HERBERT SEBASTIAN AGAR —
1897-1980, *A Time for Greatness* (Little, Brown & Co, 1942)

There are two basic parts of our mind. Our conscious mind, which is kind of the top of our head … it provides reason and judgment and discernment. Our conscious mind CAN tell the difference between a real experience and one that has been vividly imagined. However, our conscious mind, compared to the rest of our mind, is fairly useless in terms of accomplishing great things.

The rest of our mind — our subconscious mind — includes our BELIEFS, our FAITH, our COURAGE, our INSPIRATION, our EMOTIONS and our CREATIVITY. That part of us has led us out of the ice age, out of a barbaric existence into the world of abundance we live in today. And it is this part of us that can accomplish anything … electric lights, airplanes, computers, the Internet, the end of the Cold War and embracing cultural diversity. Everything we ever have accomplished (and everything we ever will) comes from this power. Call it whatever or whomever you choose. There is no denying it is there for us to use.

How many of you saw the movie *Philadelphia*? Do you remember Tom Hanks playing the part of the lawyer who contracted AIDS? Do you remember being touched by that story? Do you remember tearing up … just a little? Do you remember maybe even trying not to get emotional, but getting emotional anyway?

Do you also remember knowing all the while that this was

just a movie? Do you remember knowing that Tom was getting well paid to act the part? Do you remember knowing that he probably did not actually die, as was depicted in the movie? Did it occur to you that perhaps he never even had the dreaded disease?

This scenario demonstrates the difference between how our conscious mind "knows" things, but those things don't really matter much. And, when the powerful parts of us are subjected to a movie that moves us … it moves us. We respond as though what was playing in our head and our heart was actually real … even if we don't want to respond … we do anyway … every time.

It's true.

A vividly imagined experience has the same programming quality and impact as an actual, "real" experience.

To the powerful part of our mind, they are the exact same thing!

You see, even a real experience is no more than a perception of your mind. You have an experience and you have a perception of that experience. Your thoughts and feelings are the Vision of what that experience was for you. And, your perception is not the only true perception of that experience.

Other people who witness your experience may see something entirely different — and they frequently do.

Here's the key: You MAKE UP what happened by the thoughts and feelings you have about your experience. Think for a moment of a particular event that happened to you a long time ago — something you did which was stupid or embarrassing — something you called "a failure." Now, how many times did that particular event actually happen?

Hopefully only once. But how many times have you relived that event, vividly picturing every single detail, every thought, every feeling and sensation you experienced? Twenty or thirty times? Hundreds, perhaps thousands?

Every time you relive that one event, it has the exact same impact on you as the very first time it happened — and the exact same quality.

What do you suppose happens when you multiply that quality hundreds or even thousands of times? (And remember, in the previous example it was the quality of failure.) Can you see how easy it is to live your entire life based on the expectations you formed from that one single, isolated event?

Remember my story of stealing the sunglasses from Red's Market at the age of five, and how I learned that telling the truth was painful and humiliating? How many times do you think I relived my perception of that event? What kind of mindset do you suppose that created? Simple ... that telling the truth was a stupid and painful thing to do.

All of this — the experience itself … what you've been told about it and what you told yourself about it … the thoughts and feelings … all the pictures … the movie you created from your self-talk script … and all the times you've seen it over and over again — all of this goes together to create the beliefs you have about yourself, to create the expectations you have for your future. And, the simple, stunning secret here is …

WE MAKE IT ALL UP!

Think about that.

None of it is true. The script you are working from has nothing to do with the truth. The only real truth here is that you made it all up!

Is telling the truth really more painful than lying?

Is it true that any of us are not worthy of a loving spouse?

Is it true that anything that ever happened to you once is the way you are?

Well, yes and no. What's true is that who you are and what you will accomplish with your life is a self-fulfilling prophecy. The truth is what you choose it to be, and if you do not consciously choose, you subconsciously choose.

Most of us have been asleep at the wheel our entire adult lives. Wanting successful lives and working hard for them, only to let a miffed 5-year-old determine our destiny.

We have unknowingly used this extraordinary gift to actually live a small, quiet, safe life rarely venturing out to grab our own brand of brass ring. A few things were said and a few things happened that were so impactful that we spent the next thirty years watching those movies over and over again.

We can use this gift (and I know many of you have it) to turn our lives on a dime and produce more wellness, more aliveness, more fun, more joy, more love and more abundance in the next five years than in our last twenty. We can accomplish that by honoring this gift on purpose, and by design with some mastery of the process.

CONFIDENCE
Seeing it ...
Feeling it ...
Trusting it all.

THE ART OF DECIDING:

CONVENIENCE OR COMMITMENT

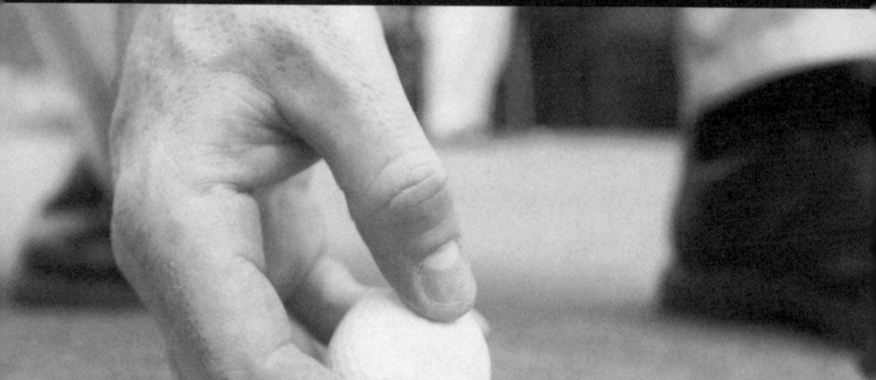

★ ★ ★ ★ ★

Whatever you can do, or dream you can, begin it. Boldness has genius, power and magic in it."

— JOHANN WOLFGANG VON GOETHE —
1749-1832, German Playwright & Philosopher

In our developmental years we form our personality. These years encompass prenatal through about age 5, and perhaps longer in children who are slow to develop emotionally. During these childhood years, without the vast background of context and reason we have as adults, we tend to experience events and *"decide" who we are versus deciding what happened*.

An example might be that as a 3-year-old you bugged Daddy to let you sit on his lap while he was reading the paper. He was stressed, tired and very interested in what he was reading. He also was not aware that the slightest discord on his part could actually lead you to form a life-long personality. So his reaction was: "NOT NOW," and it was a little stern.

You are shaken. You feel rejected. You decide in that moment:

I AM NOT ENOUGH, or
I AM NOT GOOD ENOUGH, or
I AM NOT LOVED, or
I AM NOT WORTHY OF LOVE.

This kind of "I AM-ing" is common amongst firstborns with some time before a second born; time enough for the firstborn to feel special and unique and fully loved, "UNTIL ***HE*** CAME ALONG! How dare he. Who is he? Why is he here? I must not be good enough."

This type of *decision* is not like the ones you and I make today. Nor is it a *commitment* to anything. It is an "I AM-ing." A potentially permanent decision about who you are. As I told you in my story, I made several of those decisions based on certain events. And I made others even earlier in life that made me angry and resentful.

Out of these decisions we form a personality, either to keep the decisions in place or to actually rebel against them. For example, if in the above scenario you made the decision that you were not good enough, you would either act that decision out in life, or act out proving it might not be true. Either way, the decision "not good enough" is the source of much of

▶ WEBSTER'S NEW WORLD DICTIONARY: **DECIDE**

*de.cide vt. [de-, off, from + caedere to cut] 1. to end (a contest, dispute, etc.) by giving one side the victory or by passing judgement 2. to make up one's mind or reach a decision about; determine (to decide which tie to wear) 3. to cause to reach a decision.

SYN.—decide implies the bringing to an end of vacillation, doubt, dispute, etc., by making up one's mind as to an action, course, or judgement; determine in addition suggests that the form, character, functions, scope, etc., of something are precisely fixed (the club decided on a lecture series and appointed a committee to determine the speakers, the dates, etc.); settle stresses finality in a decision, often one arrived at by arbitration, and implies the termination of all doubt or controversy; to conclude is to decide after careful investigation or reasoning; resolve implies firmness of intention to carry through a decision (he resolved to go to bed early every night).

what you do, who you associate with (marry, etc.), how you perform at work, the kind of work you do, your health and your wealth, and the quality of your relationships.

You will either succumb to it or spend your entire life trying to prove to yourself that it is not true. There is no freedom in that personality ... no peace, no authenticity and no power. Life is a constant struggle.

(*P.S. Motivating a "not good enough" who rebels against it is easy. Just tell them they can't do something, insinuating they are not good enough. They will do whatever it takes to prove you wrong. This is not healthy Motivation, but it does produce some results.*)

It is the "I AM-ing" that you will be taking on in the work of this book. Those decisions that we made early on that define us and limit us to being merely a reaction to an everyday occurrence to which, as adults, we would not give a second thought.

The "Art of Deciding" requires some distinctions.

A Decision of Who You Are

An "I AM-ing" as discussed above, is an emotional decision made one time, which in 99 percent of us is permanent for life. We make many of these by age 5, and others at key moments in our lives when we are most vulnerable or in a moment of epiphany. Perhaps during puberty, a death, a divorce or any life-shaking experience.

A Decision of Convenience

We make these kinds of decisions all the time. Something happens, or someone says something, or we encounter an opportunity and we make a decision to do something or even perhaps to become somebody more than we really are. We make these decisions because "it seems like a good idea at this time." We call this a *decision of convenience*. In the moment, it feels right and is easy. Most decisions in life are made this way. And obviously, they produce little or nothing. Why? Because what feels easy today, as you embark on any kind of change or progress, will quickly no longer feel easy or convenient. So what do we do? Of course, we decide to quit doing it.

A Decision to Commit

This is the kind of decision that produces results and permanent change. It is a decision the quality of which has long-term forward thinking to back it. It has resolve. It has a sense of "zero tolerance" for the current state of affairs. Often this quality of decision is only made when we are at the end of our rope; when we have wreaked so much havoc in our lives that we cannot stand ourselves any more ... somewhere right before a complete emotional, physical and or financial train wreck.

A decision to commit involves the distinction of commitment, which is a decision to do something NO

MATTER WHAT. It goes beyond the "JUST DO IT" slogan, to …

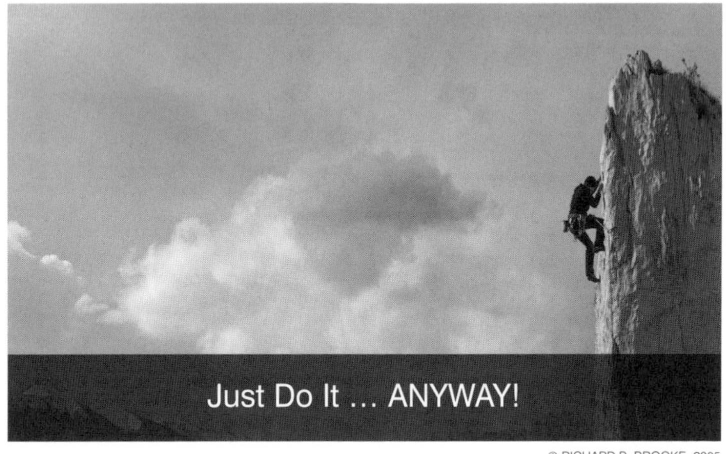

© RICHARD B. BROOKE, 2005

A commitment is a decision to do something, to be something, no matter the obstacles; no matter whether you still feel like it next week, no matter how hard it gets, no matter how many times you fail, no matter what results you are creating. A commitment pays no attention to the outcome, other than

A commitment is a Vision and a Vision is a Commitment; and as such, they cannot and will not be denied. Every power inside you, outside you and swirling in the universe — whether you call it Nature or God — is summoned to draw you to fulfill a commitment. The more committed one is, the luckier they are.

— Richard B. Brooke —

to refine strategy. Results do not alter the commitment to persevere.

So how do we make a commitment? Sometimes, especially when we cannot tolerate ourselves anymore, and sometimes when just the right mix of incentive floats by, we can make a commitment instantaneously. And waiting for either circumstance is a perilous game.

The art of making commitments is a character trait we can choose to practice. We make a commitment with the full and conscious *intention* of bringing it to fruition. And we keep making that commitment — or, if you will, returning ourselves to it over and over and over again — as often as we need to, until it takes on a course of its own or becomes part of us ... habitual.

Just making a commitment does not mean we will not have setbacks, failures and days of total despair ... days when all we can think about is how and why it makes perfect sense to forget that commitment. And if we are committed, when we are done moaning and groaning we return ourselves to our commitment and get back on track.

The most powerful place to use commitment is to change what you believe about you; to free up your spirit by letting go of a personality formed by an angry or disappointed 3-year-old. You and I can decide we are somebody different: somebody whole, somebody lovable, somebody peaceful and powerful. We can decide that because we have more to bring to the conversation than a 3-year-old. And, we have much more at stake.

In an interview with *Golf* magazine in May 2005, world-renowned golf pro Tom Lehman responded to the following questions, which perfectly illustrate the power of commitment:

What was the best advice you ever got?

The best advice ever was from Corey Pavin, in the 17th fairway at Oak Hill in the 1995 Ryder Cup. We were playing Nick Faldo and Colin Montgomerie in alternate shot, and the weather had just turned terrible. It was raining sideways and the temperature had dropped. The match was tied, and I said, "Corey, I'm so nervous I can't even breathe."

He said, "It's simple: Just get committed and swing." That's all he said, and he slapped me on the back and walked away.

COMMITMENT
Aligning mind, body and spirit in a singleness of purpose to not be denied.

The next hole, he hit a pretty good drive in the first cut of rough. They hit it in the deep stuff and had to lay up. I had a 5-iron, 205 to the pin, 185 to the front. I got committed and swung and just crushed this 5-iron right to the front part of the green, and we two-putted and won. That really sums up golf, because that commitment allows you to go ahead and make a very directed and positive swing, which leads to good shots, which lead to confidence.

You're 46. If you could go back and give young Tom Lehman advice, what would it be?

Easy: Get committed and swing. I wish I'd known Corey Pavin when I was 25.

▶ Until one is committed, there is hesitancy, the chance to draw back, always ineffectiveness. Concerning all acts of initiative (and creation) there is one elementary truth, the ignorance of which kills countless ideas and splendid plans: that the moment one definitely commits oneself, then Providence moves too. All sorts of things occur to help one that would never otherwise have occurred. A whole stream of events issues from the decision, raising in one's favor all manner of unforeseen incidents and meetings and material assistance, which no man could have dreamed would have come his way.

—William H. Murray, 1913-1996
The Scottish Himalayan Expedition
(J.M. Dent & Sons Ltd., London, 1951)

7

THE NEW SCREENPLAY

"Man is made by his belief. As he believes, so he is."

— The Bhagavad-Gita —

We made up all the beliefs we have about ourselves. We made something up based on what happened, or what we thought happened, or what someone told us happened. And then, we went about learning to believe in those stories by listening to them over and over again.

Babies don't have any beliefs. They do not believe the average person cannot earn $1,000,000 a year — yet most adults don't believe that's possible for them.

Babies do not believe in $E=mc^2$. Yet most adults do.

Babies do not have a particular religious belief. Yet most adults do, whether they understand it or not.

Babies are not racist or sexist, capitalists or communists, republicans or democrats, successes or failures. Human beings are not born believing anything.

All we are at birth is a clean slate for limitless possibilities.

So, how do we break through to access all of our dreams and aspirations?

First …

We give up our right to be right about us.

(You may want to read that again).

We give up our right to be right about us.

Most of us hold on to what we believe to be true — about life and most everything else — as if there were no possibilities for any other truth. Breaking through your barriers to success requires that you make up new ideas of what's possible, so that your possibilities support and empower your desires. It comes down to a new screenplay.

Say, for example, you currently weigh 150 pounds. You want to weigh 125, but your expectation and belief is that you weigh, and will continue to weigh, 150 pounds. How do you know what your Vision is? Pay attention to what you have been doing and eating, exercising or not.

With what you've learned so far, you know you will have to create a new expectation that you weigh 125 pounds. But that expectation will fly right in the face of what you know to be true! And, any thought other than that "truth" (that you weigh 150 pounds) will immediately seem to you to be phony or stupid. Obviously, visualizing yourself weighing 125 pounds is not true. In fact, it's a lie.

Why even suggest it? In this scenario, what's possible for us appears useless at best, and at worst, a lie. In short, there is no possibility. It's impossible!

Consider this:

The reason you do weigh 150 pounds is because you believe that's the truth. And because of that belief, you have been subtly, though powerfully, motivated — to eat just enough, laze around just enough, and justify it all just enough — to remain that way.

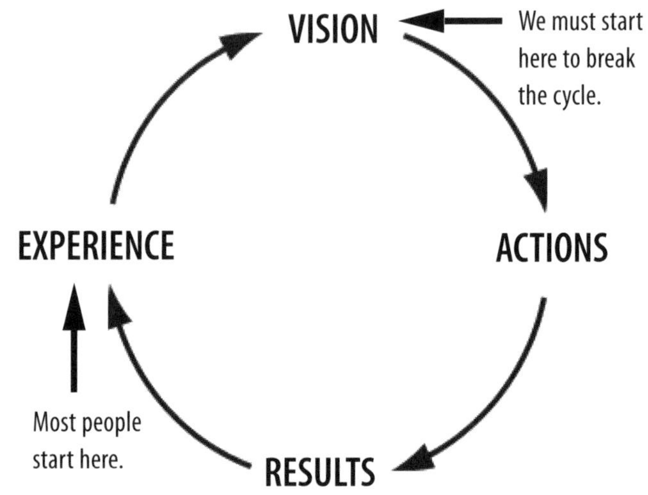

So, what can you do?

Give up your belief in yourself as a 150-pound person in exchange for the possibility of weighing 125 pounds.

Give up your right to be right in exchange for

being successful … in exchange for getting what's possible.

Creating a New Screenplay of Beliefs

Creating a new belief is like dyeing cloth in the old traditional way. Native Americans would take a piece of natural fabric and change it into a different color by soaking the cloth in a dye, squeezing it out, hanging it up to dry and set, and continuing the process over and over again until the cloth ended up the color they wanted — the color they thought was possible to achieve.

At first there was little, if any, change in the color of the fabric. It took many soakings, rinsings and settings, and the change of color was gradual. Although at times the change was hardly noticeable, the new color deepened each time. After a while, this change accelerated, becoming richer faster, until soon there was no hint of the original color. The old color was gone and in its place was the new color.

Our beliefs are created the same way. This "dyeing" process with our beliefs occurs in the mind and is known as imprinting. We have the extraordinary ability to create thoughts at will, and we can imprint those thoughts on and into our minds at will, as often as we choose — literally hundreds of times each day! Like the depth of the color of a piece of dyed cloth, we can also control the quality and intensity (i.e., power) of the imprint we create. **To the degree that our picture has clarity and detail, and can be expressed and experienced by our senses and emotions, our mind will respond to it as if it is a real experience.** The richer and more complete the image, the greater its impact in and on your mind.

Just decide to change your mind. You change your mind whenever you want to. Just do it now!

In creating new beliefs and expectations, the greater the clarity and detail, the greater the quality and power of the imprint. Let's use the ever-popular weight issue as an example of creating clarity and detail. Ask yourself these questions and answer them with as much detail and specificity as you can:

- What exactly is an excellent weight for you?
- What exactly do you look like at that weight?
- What's the shape of your body at that weight?
- Describe the new lines, curves, contours and the definition of muscles you see now?
- What do you think about when you see yourself in the mirror?
- What does the scale indicate when you step on it?
- How do your clothes fit?
- What do your new clothes look like? How do you

look wearing them?

- How do you feel at this new weight?
- Are you doing any new activities now? What do you like best about them?
- What are people saying to you about the new you?
- What are people saying about how good you look?
- How do you feel about that?
- Do you have any new attitudes?

HEALTH
The choice is with, or without.
© RICHARD B. BROOKE, 2005

- Are you more confident … more attractive … more secure … happier?

You may think that your answers to these questions sound silly, very phony or contrived. That's fine. Realize that your answers are providing a powerful clarity — your answers are filling your mind with a richness that's the equivalent of having a real life experience. In fact, because so many of us tend to sail through life, to a great degree unaware of all that's happening around us and even within us, our answers actually create a kind of "bigger and better than life" experience in our minds.

WHO ARE YOU

TO PLAY SMALL?

★★★★★

"The reasonable man adapts himself to the world … the unreasonable one persists in trying to adapt the world to himself. Therefore, all progress depends on the unreasonable man."

GEORGE BERNARD SHAW
1856-1950, Irish Dramatist

▶ WHO ARE YOU TO PLAY SMALL?

Our deepest fear is not that we are inadequate. Our deepest fear is that we are powerful beyond measure. It is our light, not our darkness, that most frightens us. We ask ourselves, "Who am I to be brilliant, gorgeous, talented or fabulous?" Actually, who are you not to be?

You are a child of God. Your playing small doesn't serve the world. There's nothing enlightened about shrinking so that other people won't feel insecure around you.

We are all meant to shine as children do. We were born to make manifest the glory of God that is within us. It's not just in some of us; it's in everyone. And as we let our own light shine, we inconspicuously give other people permission to do the same. As we are liberated from our own fear, our presence automatically liberates others.

—Marianne Williamson
A Return to Love: Reflections on the Principles of a Course in Miracles
(Random House, 1994)

Do you believe our creator would allow us to have a worthwhile desire and then not give us the ability to achieve it? That would be mockery. It would be cruel.

Dr. Napoleon Hill proved in his lifelong study of 500 of the most successful, self-made people in America (*Keys to Success: The 17 Principles of Personal Achievement*):

What the mind of man can conceive and believe, it can achieve.

Look around the world. Look at the people who are eternally happy and peaceful. Look at the 70-year-olds who compete in marathons and the elders who are living comfortably past 100. Look at the heroes and heroines who have made such a difference in our lives through their contributions. Look at our societies and world leaders. Look at the people who

PEACE
Knowing yourself. Knowing your path.
Trusting it all.

individually have made more money than some countries. The world is full of abundance, achievement, influence, respect, love and health. It is there for the borrowing. All you have to do is envision yourself with it, and it will come.

Most of us have been taught to pursue success by identifying what we want to do. We want new cars and we want to travel the world. Our tendency is to go directly for those things and the money that will provide them. And yet, our greatest point of leverage to achieve anything and everything we want is **not what we have, but who we are.** It is who we are, and who we are being in the moment, that creates the tangible results in our lives.

People who are broke or sick or friendless are so because of who they are being. What they have done to create these results is simply an effect that follows that cause.

Your version of *Mach II* has to star you. The most powerful Visions are those that redefine who you are — envisioning a person who deserves happiness, health and wealth. A person who attracts it like the powerful magnet he or she is.

To create a Vision of whom you would love to become, access these four cornerstones:

I. Your authentic values are ...

Simply those aspects of life that you treasure. What do you love about life? What must be a part of your daily life?

Examples of Values:

- Acceptance
- Appreciation
- Belonging
- Comfort
- Intimacy
- Respect
- Safety
- Security
- Fun
- Peace
- Spirituality/God
- Honesty
- Humor
- Independence
- Integrity
- Relationship
- Creativity
- Family
- Freedom
- Trust
- Work
- Communication
- Excellence
- Pleasure
- Power
- Recognition
- Joy
- Love
- Order
- Partnership
- Harmony
- Participation
- Contribution

LOVE
In the end, all we really wanted.
Give it now; accept it now.
© RICHARD B. BROOKE, 2005

For Example, the My Five Values are:

- Creativity
- Fun
- Integrity
- Love
- Success

Pick from the values listed on the previous page, or make up your own. Spend some time now identifying some of your highest authentic values. Write them down here:

1. ______________________________
2. ______________________________
3. ______________________________
4. ______________________________
5. ______________________________

II. Gifts

Each of us has one or more natural gifts or talents that are contributions to other people. You may be in denial about yours, but just ask anyone who knows you well. I believe these gifts were awarded to us for a reason — so that we can share them with the world. And, I believe that we are most powerful when we are sharing the special gifts that we are. Make sure your Visions express you sharing your gifts.

Examples of Gifts:

- Challenge
- Contribution
- Creativity
- Excellence
- Friendship
- Fun
- Honesty
- Inspiration
- Integrity
- Joy
- Leadership
- Listening
- Love
- Music
- Organization
- Spirituality
- Strength
- Success

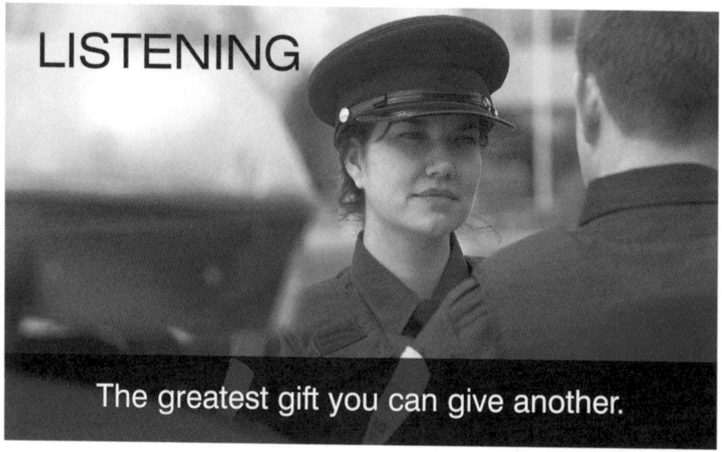

LISTENING
The greatest gift you can give another.

For Example, My Gifts are:

- Fun
- Creativity
- Leadership

Spend some time getting a sense of one of your gifts and write about it here: ______________________________

____

____

____

____

____

III. Life Purpose — or The Theme of Your Life

Your life theme is:

- Natural
- Passionate
- Joyful
- Fun
- Satisfying
- Unique to you

Each of us can discover a theme to our life. It's kind of like a song of our life, our personal purpose for being here. Life purpose is often confused with grandiose accomplishments, such as ending world hunger or discovering a cure for cancer. Although these may be authentic life purposes for somebody, for most of us the theme of our life is much simpler. For example: Raising a successful family, being a role model for the community, inspiring others to succeed — these might be authentic, powerful life purposes for many of you. Discovering and wordsmithing your life purpose is an ever-evolving project. Start now to think about it and write it into your Vision.

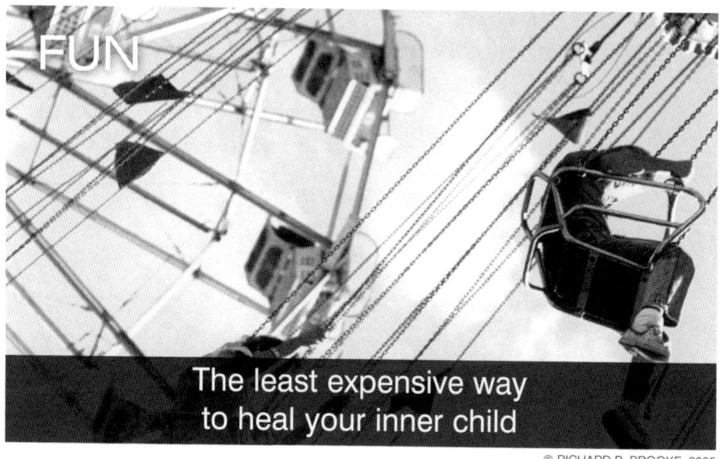
FUN
The least expensive way
to heal your inner child
© RICHARD B. BROOKE, 2005

My purpose is to live life full out, have fun, and inspire others to do the same.

What do you feel the theme of your life at its most powerful level might be? ______________________________

____

____

IV. Character Traits, Beliefs and Habits

Make a list of the ten most desired character traits, beliefs and habits that you will need to develop to become the person who attracts what you want.

Examples of Character Traits, Beliefs and Habits:

1. I act quickly on things I need to do.
2. I look for the positive and good in everyone.
3. I respect and take care of my body.
4. I deserve to be successful.
5. I play a little or a lot every day.

Add a few of your own ...

6. ______________________________
7. ______________________________
8. ______________________________
9. ______________________________
10. ______________________________

Add these character traits, beliefs and habits to your new Vision. Design your new screenplay just the way you see you will need to be to win; around who you are in your desired future. This will bring you more growth and more abundance in all areas of your life, more than any other single thing you can do.

AFFIRMATIONS

Affirmations are statements of specific goals phrased as facts. They are a way to simplify your Vision and break it into simple one-liners that can shape the way you see the world and the way you see yourself "being" in it. You may use affirmations to support your Vision. Often it is easier to read a set of affirmations throughout the day instead of the actual Vision. Do, however, read and visualize your Vision each day, once in the morning and once in the evening.

Here are some examples of affirmations:

I absolutely love myself.
I deserve happiness.
I am in action every day.
I give people my full attention.
I listen to people at a level that heals.
I am healthy and vital.
I have freedom.
I am massively productive.
I attract good fortune.
I am easy to be with.
People follow me with ease and confidence.
I ooze confidence.
I believe in me.
I know success is inevitable.
Life is fun.
I deserve abundance.
I deserve health.
I am having fun.
I love supporting people.
I love vigorous exercise.
I am wealthy.
I have lots of free time.
I get things done anyway.
I attract whatever I need.
People love listening to me.
People love being with me.
I am safe and secure.
I believe in my goals.
Life is easy.
Life is abundant.

Pick some of these or write your own. Study them daily.

As you read through this list, move past any challenge your mind brings up to an affirmation. That's just the old script, trying to tell you what you're not. You may want to read the list again.

Can you feel the power of that?

WRITING THE FILM SCRIPT OF YOUR LIFE

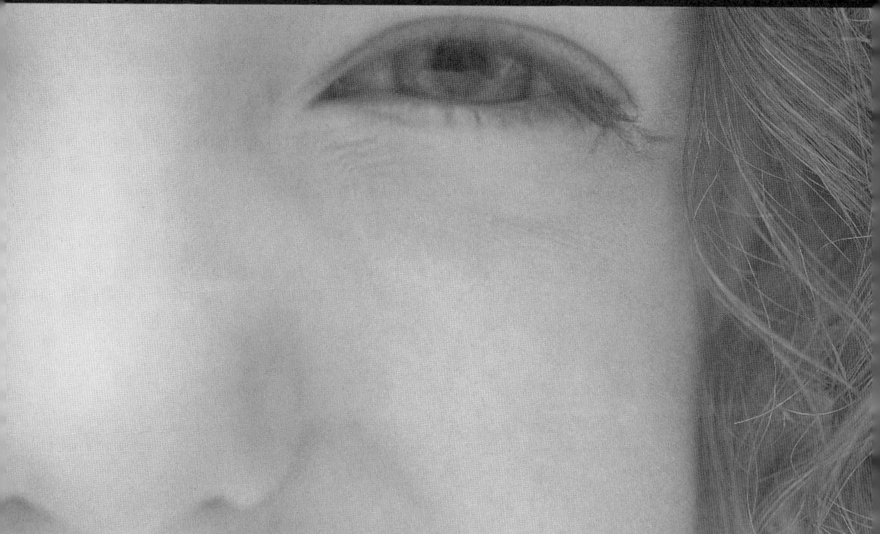

"There is more to us than we know. If we can be made to see it, perhaps for the rest of our lives we will be unwilling to settle for less."

— KURT HAHN —
1886-1974, German Educator & Philosopher

The crafting of a new Vision is best done by following the model of a film script. Film scripts are written with the specific intent to create emotions in the viewers: fear, sadness, joy, anger, glee. A great movie leads the audience to "emote" how the writer and director intended for them to emote. That is your job here; to intentionally lead yourself to experience the emotions that motivate you ... to feel how you will feel when you are actually immersed in the manifestation of your Vision.

Movies work for this because they cover the full gamut of clarity and detail. You have a detailed description in a film script of exactly what is happening and where it is happening; the seasons, the weather, the décor and the people involved. There is a soundtrack, both music to lead you to emote and dialog presented by great "actors" in such a way to lead you to emote. There are the sounds of nature, or the city, or whatever else the creative writer and director can think of that will lead you and me to feel the way they intend for us to feel.

Your NEW film script will not have any sadness, fear, anger, envy, sickness or playing small in it. You have enough of those emotions.

New Visions are simply new film scripts. So if you want to earn more money, you write a film script about you earning that specific amount of money. And since it is not money that motivates us, you will want to access the "authentic value" or "life purpose" that having more money honors. You want to ask (and keep asking) yourself: What is the underlying feeling that you are seeking? Then express that feeling the most in your new Vision or "film script."

For example, if you want to increase your income 100 percent, you need to know, more than anything else, how that will make you feel. And "good and fine" won't cut it here. You need to go deeper. Is the authentic value or life purpose to have *Freedom?* Is it to have *Independence?* Is it to have *Love?* It is to have *Power?* Is it to have *Safety?* Is it to have *Adventure?*

Check back on your authentic values. Who are you really, and what makes you stick? What is your life about, and how will doubling your income accelerate your momentum along that path?

The "secret" to change and reinvention (really the secret to success) is that the most powerful part of YOU — the most powerful being on this planet — cannot tell the difference between a real experience (the truth) and an experience that has been vividly imagined. When the most powerful collection of molecules in the universe cannot tell the difference between what we call *The Truth* and an *Imagined Truth* ... well then the Imagined Truth can become The Truth, which makes it a **self-fulfilling prophecy.**

The key to having our subconscious mind access and believe in our visualizations is to make them vivid, clear and full of every detail, including the most important detail: how we will *feel.* And we must remember the teleological nature of it. We respond to pictures quite literally. We gravitate toward what we hold in our mind, whether we want it or not.

The Rules of the Visionary's Film Script are simple and uncompromising:

1. **Describe the environment.** Where is this success taking place? Movies do not happen on white sheets of paper or in a vacuum. Set the stage. Describe the room if you are inside, the lay of the land if outside. What is the weather? Is it day or night? Hot or cold? Describe it in enough detail that your mind can fill in the blanks and paint a vivid picture of how you want the environment to *look and feel.*

2. **Describe exactly what is happening.** The shorter the experience, the easier it is to write what is happening. If you have just doubled your income, write about opening the check or depositing it, or balancing the new checkbook, or writing all the checks to pay off the bills. Avoid writing about the entire month when you doubled your income. Again, describe it in enough detail so your memory of how you *see and feel* it can fill in the blanks.

3. **Describe the soundtrack.** Will music inspire this Vision? If so, write it in and memorize the tune so you

can "dance" to it while you visualize your movie. Is nature playing one of its tunes? If so, direct it to be so.

4. **Describe the dialog.** What exactly are you saying and to whom? What are they saying to you? What are they saying to others? Write the script as you would love to have it play out. Add to every line the "tone" you intend for the "actors" to use. Is it excitement, gratitude, love, recognition, celebration?

5. **Direct the emotions.** Write into the script how you would direct the actors to play their parts. How will you act out the emotions you will experience in this Vision? How do you want others to feel about you and about what you have accomplished? How will they feel about what they have accomplished?

   The emotional part of the script is the most important because it is emotion that imprints our subconscious. It is emotions that motivate us. We want to feel a certain way and we will move mountains to feel that way. Dig deep to find the right words to describe it.

   Finding the right emotions does not necessarily mean you will "get all emotional." And when you hit it right, you will be *moved* by what you imagine yourself accomplishing and feeling.

6. **Always write in the first person.** This script is about *you* seen through *your eyes*. Language it as such: "I am this way now. I am accepting this award now."

7. **Always write in the present tense.** This is a hugely important distinction and in contrast with

goal setting. Goals are generally written as being accomplished in the future. Visions are always expressed as being accomplished right now. Not yesterday. Not tomorrow. Right now. The cognitive dissidence required to kick your subconscious into massive action will not work with a goal or a history lesson. It will only respond to what you say must be so ... right now.

8. **Always language everything as a positive word picture.** The mind responds to pictures, not words. It converts words to pictures and then pursues the pictures. If you want to quit smoking you cannot say, "I don't smoke anymore." Your mind only sees a picture of you smoking and leads you back to it. You must describe who you are and what life is like as though there is no such thing as smoking ... no word for it, no concept for it, no picture for it.

   You are not losing *weight*. You are not paying off *debts*. You are not breaking any *bad habits*. You are only expressing the new you as though those things never existed.

As you embark on the journey of writing, be patient and gentle with yourself. As you attempt to write, or even think about what to write, you are starting a process of change to your core ... change that you may have not ever have attempted before. You have 20, 30, 40, maybe 80 years invested in who you are. You will not take kindly to changing overnight.

Start with your **Authentic Values**, your **Gifts** and what you feel might be the **Theme of Your Life**. Think about what you would like to do along those lines; what you would like to have, and most importantly, who you want to become. Success comes *through* us before it comes *to* us. Your greatest leverage to a new life is to shift who you are: your habits, your character traits, your beliefs about you and other people. You were not born with any of those "qualities." You adopted them and you can replace them at will any time you choose.

The most pivotal Visions are those that address the issues to tell a vivid and rewarding story of WHO THE NEW YOU IS.

Use the affirmations on page 133 (Chapter 8: *Who Are You to Play Small*). Use your newfound Authentic Values, Gifts and the Theme of your Life. Start writing a story of a moment in time when you are someone more powerful, more confident, more compassionate, more open, more vulnerable, and most of all much, much more successful in whatever arena you choose.

Write and read. Read and visualize. Visualize and feel … and with the feelings will come movement.

10

SHOOTING MACH II

★★★★★

"It is what you choose NOT to see in your life that controls your life."

— Lynn V. Andrews —
Best-selling Author, Mystic & Spiritual Leader

Seeing is believing. Every picture tells a story and it's true that each picture is worth a thousand words. You will want to use photo illustrations (whether you take them yourself or clip them from magazines) to create powerful images — pictures that support your Vision.

Magnetic photo albums are perfect for this purpose. Clip pictures from magazines that accurately describe the possibilities as you see them in your future, and assemble them creatively on the pages of your "Vision Book."

If you want your body to look a certain way, check out fitness magazines for pictures of you as you want to be. Clip pictures of clothes you desire from fashion magazines; vacation spots you want to visit from travel magazines; the car you want; the stereo; grown-up toys; anything and everything that accurately and artfully represents the things you desire to have, do, or be, and paste those pictures into your book. You can max out the power of these images by literally putting yourself in the picture. If there's a particular car you long for, take a camera to the dealer, select the make, model, color, etc., of the car of your choice, and have the salesperson snap a couple shots of you in the driver's seat. Paste that picture in your book.

If there's an outfit you desire that you've clipped from a magazine, cut out a picture of your head and paste it over the model's face. You can do this with a house, a muscular body, a scene from a distant land, an activity such as driving a race car, skydiving … anything.

Also, many magazines have sections devoted to up-and-comers, such as hot new names on the business scene, etc. You can easily create the words and pictures that list you as the subject of these articles. Put these in your book as well.

Make up a paycheck and write the weekly or monthly income you desire on it and paste that in. And, don't forget headlines and captions. Research has shown the headline of an advertisement and the captions under photographs are the most read and remembered elements of the ad. Make up your own positive, descriptive captions for your pictures.

Actor and comedian Jim Carrey wrote himself a check for $10 million when he was at one of his lowest points. He signed it "for acting services rendered."

Magazines are filled with powerful, positive headlines that you can cut out and use to give your Vision Book the one-two punch of both words and pictures.

Go on with this, making it richer and incorporating more specific elements that are unique to you and your own life circumstances.

The point is to add as much detail; as many rich, sensory ingredients; and as much passion, emotion and enthusiasm as possible. And again, avoid completely any mention of what you don't want.

You can dramatically increase the quantity of the imprints

your mind receives — and therefore, their quality and power as well — simply by listening to your own self-talk, self-image audio cassette tape. The script should be along the lines of the previous example, but of course, it's your own, "customized" version. You can burn your own compact disk or MP3 to accomplish the same thing.

Compose your script and read it into your tape recorder. Put on your best, most enthusiastic radio announcer's voice when you make your recording. Then play it back when you're riding in the car, doing mundane chores, working out, especially just before you go to sleep … any time and every time you have the opportunity. Your script played over and over again will each time create a fresh, brand-new image imprint in your mind.

Remember, you create and deepen all of your beliefs by reliving those experiences over and over in your feeling mind. Listening to your self-talk tape is a powerful way to imprint and readjust the balance scales in your mind, in favor of the new self-image you now envision.

Now that you've got all of this wonderful stuff, what do you do with it?

At least twice every day — and more often if you will make the time — read your script or listen to your tape, look at your book and visualize yourself, fully, richly and completely living your Vision and loving it.

Allow yourself to feel how you will feel when you are

enjoying your success. The best times for doing this are when you first wake up in the morning and just before you drift off to sleep at night. That sort of waking-dreaming state is one where your mind is super receptive to the imprinting process.

Each time you read, look or listen to any of this material, make sure you are as relaxed and comfortable as possible. Of course, you can listen while exercising or doing some repetitive or "mindless" activity, but it is best done when you're quiet, alone and relaxed. That's when you're most open and receptive, and it's also when the feeling-awareness of your mind is clear of distractions, which allows it to be its most creative.

Here's a very important caution:

Initially, you may reject these images in your imprinting process as false or foolish, or you might make some other critical interpretation or judgment about them. DO NOT fight these reactions. When they surface, simply thank yourself for expressing that opinion and replace those criticisms with your positive visualizations. Remember, you make it all up anyway, so why not make up thoughts that empower you?

Just continue to go back to your visualizations no matter how many times you may be derailed by your old "judgmental" beliefs. Just do it anyway. Remember, if you don't change your

Vision, your old Vision will still dominate. So, you are doing it anyway, just do it differently.

Any new Vision can become real to you just by following the screenwriter's model, sometimes expressed in three questions:

1. What exactly is happening?

2. What exactly are people saying and how are they saying it?

3. How are you feeling?

With that captured, simply write the screenplay of your life:

1. Write a film script in exact detail.

2 Write it as though it is happening NOW.

3. Write it in the first person: "I am now experiencing this…"

4. Specifically write:

- What you are doing.
- What you are saying.
- What you are feeling.
- What others are doing.
- What others are saying.
- What others are feeling.

5. Avoid any words labeling what you don't want, like:

- Stop **smoking.**
- Lose **fat.**
- Pay off **debts.**

6. Secure pictures that help tell the story.

As you visualize, allow yourself to see, hear, sense and especially feel — physically, intellectually and emotionally as well — just the way you would as if you were actually living the experience here and now. Take at least several minutes for each different image you are visualizing. Throughout your day, whenever and wherever you can, create the opportunity to reflect on your Vision. Place pictures on your mirror, by your phone, beside your bed, on the ceiling, in the car, above your television — better yet, tape it right over the television screen! Cover your world with these vivid and powerful reminders of your future.

In time, your new Vision will become a habit. It will flow into, around and through your mind without you even having to think about it. How long this takes depends solely on the quality of your images and the quantity of the imprints themselves. It may take you weeks, a month, three months or a year. It will probably only take you a few days to begin to see the first positive results. Rest assured, your Vision will take hold!

This method has NEVER failed anyone who has done it consistently. The imprinting process may work quickly for you or slowly for you, but if you stick with it, it will work for sure. The only way the imprinting process will not work is if you quit. If you quit, then it will start again with your old Vision.

As your new Vision TAKES hold your mindset will elevate, creating that subtle, yet powerful Motivation, which will positively impact all your actions and behaviors. Your performance in nearly every area of your life and work will change for the better. You will notice that you possess more and more Courage … Enthusiasm … Confidence … Persistence … Passion … Desire … and Commitment … all of which are guaranteed to move your reality steadily and inevitably toward your possibilities.

You will break through your barriers to success. You will experience the movie, *Mach II With Your Hair On Fire!*

Perhaps this all sounds pretty silly to you. Perhaps you're thinking it might be a fun project, but does it really work? Can it really work for someone like you? Believe me. It's not silly — and it absolutely does work, and it will work for you.

The Movie of Your Life

Since real experiences play in your memory like a movie, you'll want the Vision you create to be just like a movie as well. Write a film script of a moment in your life when you are who you would love to be.

Your film script will include a full and complete description of the sets and props — the location and lighting for each and every scene. The script also includes dialog — all the conversations that are taking place, plus all the real-time action, and even how all the people in your movie think and feel about everything that's going on.

Two keys to creating a successful film script imprint include making all of your dialogs **present tense** and **positive.** Your mind absorbs what you imagine literally, exactly as you imagine it. Therefore, your film script must be crafted so that all your possibilities are already achieved and in your possession right now. For example: the statement, "I *will* weigh 'X' pounds," only serves to confirm that you're still

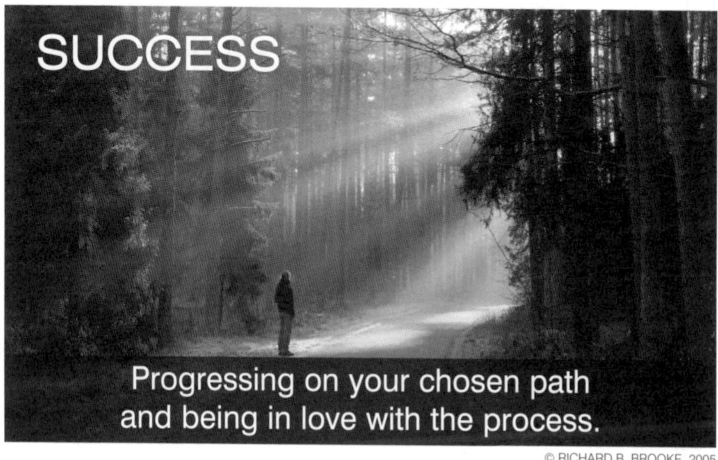
SUCCESS
Progressing on your chosen path
and being in love with the process.

overweight.

Tomorrow is the only day which never comes, yet for most people that's the only place and time their accomplishments and aspirations ever exist. The best you can get from this kind of would-be, should-be dialog is to affirm that you're a fat person who wants to be thin … a failure, falling short of success.

Remember, desire alone doesn't cut it. So, make sure your imprint is always in the present tense.

Wordsmithing Your Vision

1. **All phrases are positive.**
2. **All phrases are present tense.**
3. **Phrases describing you are written in the first person — I or we.**
4. **Clarity gives the Vision power. Give the details of your Vision.**
5. **Emotions, tone and energy provide clarity. Write about the emotions, the tone and the energy.**

Another key is to keep it positive. Dialog or conversation brings up pictures in our mind. So, immediately after our mind receives a negative message, such as "I don't smoke cigarettes anymore," what does it do? Right, there's the picture of you smoking.

Instead, create a positive image of what it's like for you to be free of smoking.

For example:

"*My car, my home, my clothes and my breath smell clean and fresh. I am tasting new and fantastic flavors in all the foods I eat. I breathe fully, deeply, and every breath I take gives me increased energy and makes me more and more happy and alive! I am healthy! I am in control! I am free!"*

Do you get the difference between that imprint and, "I don't smoke cigarettes anymore?" Stay away from negative images by using only positive phraseology (i.e., don't use "don't").

▶ GOALS VERSUS VISIONS

The more people read about Vision and the Motivation it produces, the more their traditional training about goals seems at odds with it. Let me assure you it is not. Goals are a very valuable technology for "focusing the mind" (Vision). Written goals have been documented to be 10 to 100 times more effective than "thinking you are thinking" about them.

Goals rely on several things that Visions do not rely upon.

Goals rely on deadlines. Deadlines can be very valuable. They create a sense of urgency, reducing procrastination. People who get committed to the deadlines within their goals — and are empowered by those deadlines — find they can produce more in a few days than the same person would normally produce in a few months.

Some people may be disempowered by deadlines. The looming date creates self-talk like: "I can't hit this deadline." In these cases, deadlines are not powerful.

Goals also rely on strategies or plans. Plans are important and anyone can tell you that the plan you start with is not usually the plan with which you end. Plans change ... sometimes overnight.

If you have a short-term goal and you feel like a deadline empowers you, by all means write out the goal and include the deadline. However, this is not a Vision. Often deadlines are there whether we want them or not, as in contests or end-of-the-business-month cycles. Longer term goals are not well served with deadlines, as without the deadline you may have achieved it earlier. If you do write out a goal for a short-term deadline objective, also write out a Vision of you already in possession of it or having achieved it. Use both tools (goals and Visions) to get you there.

One of the challenges with deadlines is they are, in themselves, an affirmation that you do not currently own or possess what it is you want. You are affirming you will get it, which affirms you do not have it. The mind does not respond well to what you say you want, or even to what you say you will get. It responds to what you say is so NOW, and how that NOW contrasts with what you have. The contrast produces Motivation to close the gap.

Plans are valuable and a motivated person will create and keep creating a plan until it works. A motivated person does not worry about the "how," as they know the how will come. Creativity (Motivation) will create the how.

Create the Motivation and everything else you need — money, people, plans, ideas — will either be created by you, or it will be attracted to you.

Goal setting is an effective tool due to the way the mind captures and processes the goal. However, the way the goal is phrased versus the way a Vision is phrased makes goals vastly less effective for inspiring what it takes (Motivation) to get it done. Always use a Vision and if deadlines empower you, use them for short-term objectives.

▶ "CINDERELLA STORY" NOW CLASSIC

Columnist Tom Clark recounted the following classic movie moment in an article that appeared in USA Today in April 2001:

The 1980 movie Caddyshack has become a comedy classic. No scene is more memorable than that of assistant greenskeeper, Carl Spackler, played brilliantly by actor Bill Murray, when he fantasizes about playing for The Masters championship while he swings at flowers with a hoe.

The following text is spoken by Murray, as Carl the greenskeeper, verbatim from the movie:

"What an incredible Cinderella story, this unknown comes outta nowhere to lead the pack, at Augusta. He's on his final hole, he's about 455 yards away — he's gonna hit about a 2-iron I think.

"Oh he got all of that one! The crowd is standing on its feet here, the normally reserved Augusta crowd — going wild — for this young Cinderella, he's come outta nowhere, he's got about 350 yards left, he's gonna hit about a 5-iron, don't you think?

"He's got a beautiful backswing that's — oh, he got all of that one! He's gotta be pleased with that, the crowd is just on its feet here, uh — he's the Cinderella boy, uh — tears in his eyes I guess as he lines up this last shot, he's got about 195 yards left, he's got about a — it looks like he's got about an 8-iron.

"This crowd has gone deathly silent, the Cinderella story, outta nowhere, a former greenskeeper now — about to become The Masters champion.

"It looks like a mirac... It's in the hole!"

—Tom Clark
USA Today (April 2001)

▶ THE FOLLOWING ARE SOME EXAMPLES OF VISIONS.

Study how they "create" a Vision of success.

I weigh ______ pounds and I'm loving every minute of it! I look fantastic!

It's great to fit into size ___ clothes that fit me perfectly and hang so beautifully from my trim, sculpted body.

I swim and sunbathe in the luxury of my new freedom. As I walk down the beach, people turn and say, "Look at ________, (use your own name) what a great body!"

I love the way I look and so does everyone else!

I'm more active than ever before. I'm doing things most 20-year-olds can't do! I bike, play tennis and enjoy working out. When the aerobics teacher asks who is the most improved person in class, everybody shouts, "________ is!"

My friends say ______'s the most healthy and fit person they know. And they're right! I'm so proud of my lifestyle — and what's more, I'm proud to have turned so many people on to eating light and right, being vital and alive, fit and trim, looking and feeling terrific! People are calling me "The Ambassador of Health." They love me for it — and I love it, too.

I am a sterling example of health and creative power for everyone I meet!

I'm making a positive difference in so many people's lives.

▶ SAMPLE VISION

Life just got a lot easier.

Today good fortune and abundance is showering upon me. I now have the financial freedom and independence that I so richly deserve. And now I have the free time to enjoy it. Now I travel ... to the exotic places of the world and I do so in total comfort and ease. I love the vibrancy of South America. I can hear the music and I can feel the vibes. The people here are so happy ... so grateful and so loving. This place renews me! I love the Caribbean. The islands, the warm soft sand, the laid-backness of it all. And the water ... a trillion gallon bathtub full of live toys. I could sleep here forever.

I can enjoy these places because I have secured wealth now. It flows and flows and flows. Tens of thousands of dollars in net income lifts me up and carries me wherever I choose to go. I love first class. I love service. I love the freedom of no-limit fun.

These rich rewards come to me out of my development. My passion for my business. My passion for people and their goals. My passion for the abundance life has stored up for all of us. I am now the person others go to for love, for guidance, for coaching and for leadership. I am the go-to gal and I love it! I feel the freedom. I hear the silence of the ocean 30 feet under. I hear the rhythm of the music. I hear the laughter of friends and loved ones "being" here too. I feel the joy. I feel the safety. I feel the warmth. This is what I have always wanted and, most importantly, learned to expect. Fun, Freedom, Friends and Family. I am all in.

11

SUCCESS

★★★★★

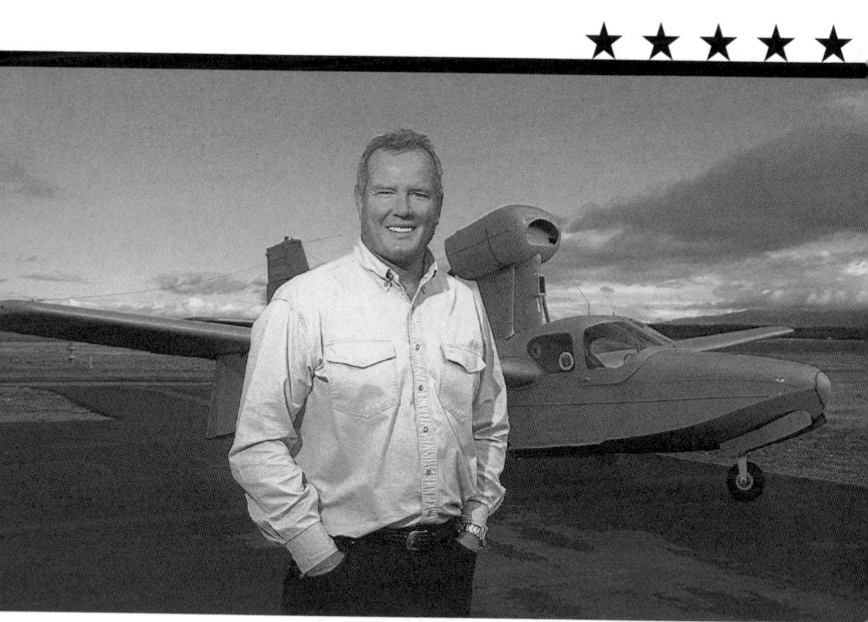

"The important thing is this: to be ready at any moment to sacrifice what we are for what we could become."

— CHARLES DUBOIS —
1847-1885, American Artist

In 1983, I purchased a mock-up of the cover of *SUCCESS* magazine with my picture on the cover. I framed it and hung it on my wall and looked at it every day. My Vision at that time was to be not only rich, but famous as well. I wanted something to prove to my friends and family that I really was cutting it. *SUCCESS* magazine seemed like the perfect proof.

In March 1992 (almost ten years later), *SUCCESS* magazine featured the Network Marketing industry's skyrocketing success as its lead story. It was the first time a mainstream publication had done so in the industry's 50-year history. Out of 10 million Network Marketers, they chose me for the cover and lead story.

A mocked-up cover of *SUCCESS* magazine that I purchased at a fair in Ohio, May 1983.

Now, you may think this happened because I was the most outspoken, flamboyant, successful or famous person in the industry — not at all. Or, perhaps you think it was because I hired some public relations firm to make it happen. I didn't.

Actually, and rightfully so, *SUCCESS* wanted Rich DeVos, president of the $6-billion-a-year Amway Corporation on the cover. He has created thousands of millionaires. He and his partner Jay Van Andel have built the number one Network Marketing organization in the world and they are five, (count them!) five times bigger than number two! *SUCCESS* magazine thought he should be on the cover. He, however, did not return *SUCCESS*'s phone call. You may think he did not return their call because he was too busy, or he didn't care. I don't think so. Rich DeVos did not return that call for only one reason … I had the picture of myself on that cover. He, obviously, did not.

The Hidden Psychology Behind Good Customer Service

SUCCESS

THE MAGAZINE FOR TODAY'S ENTREPRENEURIAL MIND

34 MASTERS OF MULTI-LEVEL MARKETING PROCLAIM:

"WE CREATE MILLIONAIRES"

Their Eager Disciples Build Overnight Empires

Lightning Growth: He Recruited Friends and Made $500 Million.

Sizzling Sales: His Oxyfresh Team Soared to Riches.

Wave of the Future: He Teaches MLM Tactics to Major Corporations.

CONQUER COMPLEX PROJECTS

Now, a New Generation of Tools and Techniques

PLUS

Ax Your Taxes: The Sharpest New Software

Attack Big Companies: Seize Their Niches

Actual March 1992 cover of *SUCCESS* magazine. This issue outsold every issue in the 100-year history of the magazine.

▶ MACH II SUCCESS TIPS

Keep these tips and notes as a handy reference:

One of my Visions is for tens of millions of people to carry their most vital Vision statements on them, just like their driver's license or a credit card. Thank you for starting the journey of becoming a Card Carrying Visionary. I would love to hear your success stories.

1. A Vision is how you see, hear and feel yourself performing any given "goal."

2. Goals are not Visions, but Visions are goals. Goals are statements of what you want. Visions are statements affirming you now have it and affirming how it will make you feel. Visions are vastly more powerful than goals.

3. Replace your current Visions with ones that match your goals.

4. You already have a Vision for everything you can imagine yourself doing.

5. You will be motivated to the degree you "envision" a performance that contrasts with how you currently perform.

6. Motivation looks like enthusiasm, courage, physical energy, creativity and persistence.

7. Creativity is problem solving and, most importantly, "creative interpretations" or "green lights."

8. You can train yourself to believe your Visions through spaced repetition of "watching the movie."

9. Visions initially are best written as statements or affirmations.

10. Each statement must be written in the first person and each statement must use only positive word pictures.

11. Example of what does not work: I am losing 20 pounds; or I am quitting smoking; or I am paying off all my debt. The word pictures the mind focuses on are 20 pounds, smoking and debt.

12. Examples of what does work: I now weigh 120 pounds and look fabulous in my new size 4 outfits. I love the new fresh, clean, healthy me. I smell great. I sleep great. I feel great and I am an inspiration to those around me. I love the freedom of financial success and wisdom. My credit score is 780. I am now saving money every month and it is compounding away!

13. Create lists of things you want to do; things you want to have and, most importantly, things you want to BE. When we become a more valuable person, all other rewards will come.

14. Visualize your new Visions every day — especially first thing in the morning and the last thing before sleep.

15. Look for ways to put your Visions into action. You will see opportunities you did not see before and, more importantly, you will find a natural inclination to act on them. This is Motivation at work. You will also begin to "vibrate," if you will, at a level that attracts people, circumstances and conditions that will support you in manifesting your Visions.

ON INSPIRATION

★ ★ ★ ★ ★

I am a great believer in the power of inspiration to influence our own powerful Visions. The following are some of my favorites. Reading and reflecting on their wisdom allows me to feel the way I feel when I'm starring in the movie of my life. I encourage you to find and reflect on everything and anything that does the same for you.

— Richard B. Brooke —

▶ THE INVITATION

It doesn't interest me what you do for a living. I want to know what you ache for, and if you dare to dream of meeting your heart's longing.

It doesn't interest me how old you are. I want to know if you will risk looking like a fool for love, for your dream, for the adventure of being alive.

It doesn't interest me what planets are squaring your moon … I want to know if you have touched the center of your own sorrow, if you have been opened by life's betrayals, or have become shriveled and closed from fear of further pain.

I want to know if you can sit with pain, mine or your own, without moving to hide it, or fade it or fix it.

I want to know if you can be with joy, mine or your own, if you can dance with wildness and let the ecstasy fill you to the tips of your fingers and toes without cautioning us to be careful, to be realistic, to remember the limitations of being human.

It doesn't interest me if the story you're telling me is true. I want to know if you can disappoint another to be true to yourself. If you can bear the accusation of betrayal, and not betray your own soul. If

This, therefore, is a faded dream of the time when I went down into the dust and noise of the eastern marketplace, with my brain and muscles, with sweat and constant thinking, made others see my Visions coming true. Those who dream by night in the dusty recesses of their minds wake in the day to find that all was vanity, but the dreamers of the day are dangerous men, for they may act their dream with open eyes, and make it possible.

— T.E. Lawrence, 1888-1935
Introduction to Seven Pillars of Wisdom, (Oxford Edition, 1922)

you can be faithless and therefore trustworthy.

I want to know if you can see Beauty even when it's not pretty every day. And if you can source your own life from its presence.

I want to know if you can live with failure, yours and mine, and still stand at the edge of a lake and shout to the silver of the full moon, "Yes."

It doesn't interest me to know where you live or how much money you have. I want to know if you can get up after the night of grief and despair; weary and bruised to the bone, and do what needs to be done to feed the children.

It doesn't interest me who you know, or how you came to be here. I want to know if you will stand in the center of the fire with me and not shrink back.

It doesn't interest me where, or what or with whom, you have studied. I want to know what sustains you from the inside, when all else falls away.

I want to know if you can be alone with yourself, and if you truly like the company you keep in the empty moments.

— Oriah Mountain Dreamer
The Invitation, (Harper San Francisco, 1999)

The Masters in the art of living make little distinction between their work and their play, their labor and their leisure, their minds and their bodies, their information and their recreation, their love and their religion.

They simply pursue their VISION OF EXCELLENCE at whatever they do, leaving others to decide whether they are working or playing. To them, they are always doing both!

— James A. Mitchner, 1907-1997
Pulitzer Prize Winning Novelist

If I feel depressed, I will sing.
If I feel sad, I will laugh.
If I feel ill, I will double my labor.
If I feel fear, I will plunge ahead.
If I feel poverty, I will think of wealth to come.
If I feel incompetent, I will remember past success.
If I feel insignificant, I will remember my goals.
Today I will be the master of my emotions.

— Og Mandino, 1923-1996
The Greatest Salesman in the World, (Bantam; Reissued Edition, 1983)

• • • • •

Carefully watch your thoughts, for they become your words.
Manage and watch your words, for they will become your actions.
Consider and judge your actions, for they have become your habits.
Acknowledge and watch your habits, for they shall become your values.
Understand and embrace your values, for they become your destiny.

— Mahatma Gandhi, 1869-1948

• • • • •

Forces that threaten to negate life must be challenged by courage, which is the power of life to affirm itself in spite of life's ambiguities. This requires the exercise of a creative will that enables us to hew out a stone of hope from a mountain of despair.

— Martin Luther King, Jr., 1929-1968
Strength to Love, (Harper & Row, 1963)

If we don't change our direction, we are likely to end up where we are headed.

— Chinese Proverb

• • • • •

Amidst the glut of insignificance that engulfs us all, the temptation is understandable to stop thinking. The trouble is that unthinking persons cannot choose, but must let others choose for them. To fail to make one's own choices is to betray the freedom which is our society's greatest gift to all of us.

— Stephen Muller,
President Emeritus, Johns Hopkins University

• • • • •

Every creative act involves ... a new innocence of perception, liberated from the cataract of accepted belief.

— Arthur Koestler, 1905 - 1983
The Sleepwalkers, (Hutchinson, 1959)

There are many who are living far below their possibilities because they are continually handing over their individualities to others. Do you want to be a power in the world? Then be yourself. Be true to the highest within your soul and then, allow yourself to be governed by no customs or conventionalities or arbitrary man-made rules that are not founded on principle.

— Ralph Waldo Trine, 1866 - 1958
In Tune With the Infinite, (Kessinger Publishing, 1910 Edition)

• • • • •

▶ THE FOUR AGREEMENTS

1. BE IMPECCABLE WITH YOUR WORD

Speak with integrity. Say only what you mean. Avoid using the word to speak against yourself or to gossip about others. Use the power of your word in the direction of truth and love.

2. DON'T TAKE ANYTHING PERSONALLY

Nothing others do is because of you. What others say and do is a projection of their own reality, their own dream. When you are immune to the opinions and actions of others, you won't be the victim of needless suffering.

3. DON'T MAKE ASSUMPTIONS

Find the courage to ask questions and to express what you really want. Communicate with others as clearly as you can to avoid misunderstandings, sadness and drama. With just this one agreement, you can completely transform your life.

4. ALWAYS DO YOUR BEST

Your best is going to change from moment to moment; it will be different when you are healthy, as opposed to sick. Under any circumstance, simply do your best, and you will avoid self-judgment, self-abuse and regret.

— DON MIGUEL RUIZ
The Four Agreements, (Amber-Allen Publishing, © 1997)
Used with permission.

▶ THE DASH

I read of a man who stood to speak at the funeral of a friend.

He referred to the dates on her tombstone; her life from beginning to end (1934-1998).

He noted that first came her date of birth and spoke the ending date with tears, but he said what mattered most of all was the dash between those years.

For that dash represents all the time that she spent alive on earth ... And now, only those who loved her know what that little line is worth.

For it matters not how much we own; the cars ... the house ... the cash, what matters is how we live and love and how we spend our dash.

So think about this long and hard ... are there things you'd like to change? For you never know how much time is left, that can still be rearranged.

If we could just slow down enough to consider what's true and real, and always try to understand the way other people feel.

And be less quick to anger, and show appreciation more, and love the people in our lives like we've never loved before.

If we treat each other with respect, and more often wear a smile ... Remembering that this special dash might only last a little while.

So, when your eulogy's being read, your life's actions to rehash ... Would you be proud of what they'll say about how you spent your dash?

— Linda Ellis (www.lindaellis.net)
The Dash © 1998, Linda Ellis
Used with permission.

▶ ALL I EVER REALLY NEEDED TO KNOW I LEARNED IN KINDERGARTEN

Most of what I really need to know about how to live, and what to do, and how to be, I learned in Kindergarten. Wisdom was not at the top of the graduate school mountain, but there in the sandbox at nursery school.

These are the things I learned ...

Share everything.
Play fair.
Don't hit people.
Put things back where you found them.
Clean up your own mess.
Don't take things that aren't yours.
Say sorry when you hurt somebody.
Wash your hands before you eat.
Flush.
Warm cookies and cold milk are good for you.
Live a balanced life.

Learn some and think some and draw and paint and sing and dance and play and work every day some.

Take a nap every afternoon.

When you go out into the world, watch for traffic, hold hands, and stick together.

Be aware of wonder. Remember the little seed in the plastic cup? The roots go down and the plant goes up and nobody really knows how or why, but we are all like that.

Goldfish and hamsters and white mice and even the little seed in the plastic cup — they all die. So do we.

And then remember the book about Dick and Jane and the first word you learned, the biggest word of all: LOOK.

Everything you need to know is in there somewhere.

The Golden Rule and love and basic sanitation.

Ecology and politics and sane living.

Think of what a better world it would be if we all — the whole world had cookies and milk about 3 o'clock every afternoon and then lay down with our blankets for a nap. Or if we had a basic policy in our nation and other nations to always put things back where we found them and cleaned up our own messes. And it is still true, no matter how old you are, when you go out into the world, it is best to hold hands and stick together.

—Robert Fulghum
Best-selling Author, www.robertfulghum.com, 1988

A midlife crisis is when you've reached the top rung of your ladder only to realize that you've leaned it against the wrong wall.

— AUTHOR UNKNOWN

• • • • •

Far better it is to dare mighty things, win glorious triumphs, even though checkered by failure, than to rank with those poor spirits who neither enjoy much nor suffer much, because they live in the gray twilight that knows no victory or defeat.

— THEODORE ROOSEVELT, 1858 - 1919
From the speech, *The Strenuous Life,* (Chicago; April 10, 1899)

• • • • •

... I think it is a mistake to ever look for hope outside of one's self. One day the house smells of fresh bread, the next of smoke and blood. One day you faint because the gardener cuts his finger off, within a week you're climbing over corpses of children bombed in a subway. What hope can there be if that is so? I tried to die near the end of the war. The same dream returned each night until I dared not to sleep and grew quite ill. I dreamed I had a child, and even in the dream I saw it was my life, and it was an idiot and ran away. But it always crept onto my lap again clutched at my clothes. Until I thought, if I could kiss it whatever it was my own, perhaps I could sleep. And I bent to its broken face and it was horrible ... but I kissed it. I think one must finally take one's life in one's arms ....

— ARTHUR MILLER, 1915 - 2005
From the play, *After the Fall,* (1964)

When one door closes another door opens; but we so often look so long and so regretfully upon the closed door, that we do not see the ones which open for us.

— Alexander Graham Bell, 1847-1922
American Scientist & Inventor

• • • • •

A pessimist sees the difficulty in every opportunity. An optimist sees the opportunity in every difficulty.

— Winston S. Churchill, 1874-1965
British Prime Minister

• • • • •

Surrender does not mean being passive; it means engaging yourself totally in what you are doing and then letting go of the outcome.

— Yogi Amrit Desai
Doctor of Yoga and Holistic Healing

• • • • •

Security is mostly superstition. It does not exist in nature. Nor do the children of men as a whole experience it. Avoiding danger is no safer in the long run than outright exposure. Life is either a daring adventure or nothing at all.

— Helen Keller, 1880-1968
The Open Door, (Doubleday and Company, 1957)

THE LAW OF RESPONSIBILITY

Once we establish the limits and boundaries of our responsibility, we can take full charge of that which is our duty and let go of that which is not; in doing so, we find more enjoyment supporting others, as we create more harmonious cooperative relationships by understanding that which falls within the realm of our responsibility.

— DAN MILLMAN
Excerpt from *The Life You Were Born to Live,* (HJ Kramer, 1993)

• • • • •

People, like nails, lose their effectiveness when they lose direction and begin to bend.

— WALTER SAVAGE LANDOR, 1775 - 1864
English Poet

• • • • •

People should follow their own energy.

— WILL SCHULTZ, 1902 - 1998
American Economist

• • • • •

If at the end ... I have lost every other friend on earth, I shall at least have one friend left, and that friend shall be down inside of me.

— ABRAHAM LINCOLN, 1809 - 1865
16th President of the United States

We cannot put off living until we are ready. The most salient characteristic of life is its coerciveness: it is always urgent, "here and now" without any possible postponement. Life is fired at us point-blank.

— José Ortega y Gasset, 1883 - 1955
Spanish Philosopher

• • • • •

I have found the best way to give advice to your children is to find out what they want and then advise them to do it.

— Harry S. Truman, 1884 - 1972
33rd President of the United States

• • • • •

With dedication to the rights of humanity with the empowerment of listening integrated with this Chinese philosophy that: "There's nothing noble in being superior to someone else. The true nobility is in being superior to your previous self."

— Reverend Peikang Dai

• • • • •

It is not because things are difficult that we do not dare, it is because we do not dare that things are difficult.

— Seneca, 5BC - 65AD
Roman Philosopher

▶ THE OPTIMIST CREED

Promise yourself ...

To be so strong that nothing can disturb your peace of mind.

To talk health, happiness and prosperity to every person you meet.

To make all your friends feel that there is something to them.

To look at the sunny side of everything and make your optimism come true.

To think only the best, to work for the best and expect only the best.

To be just as enthusiastic about the success of others as you are about your own.

To forget the mistakes of the past and press on to the greater achievements of the future.

To wear a cheerful countenance at all times and to give every living creature you meet a smile.

To give so much time to the improvement of yourself that you have no time to criticize others.

To be too large for worry, too noble for anger, too strong for fear and too happy to permit the presence of trouble.

— CHRISTIAN D. LARSON

Your Forces and How to Use Them, (LN Fowler & Co, Ltd.; London, 1912)

You can be right or you can be happy.

— Gerald G Jampolsky, M.D.
Founder, Center for Attitudinal Healing, (Sausalito, California)

• • • • •

For peace of mind, we need to resign as general manager of the universe.

— Larry Eisenberg

• • • • •

To-morrow, and to-morrow, and to-morrow,
Creeps in this petty pace from day to day,
To the last syllable of recorded time;
And all our yesterdays have lighted fools
The way to dusty death. Out, out, brief candle!
Life is but a walking shadow; a poor player,
That struts and frets his hour upon the stage,
And then is heard no more: it is a tale
told by an idiot, full of sound and fury,
Signifying nothing.

— William Shakespeare, 1564 - 1616
From the play, *Macbeth*

• • • • •

Success seems to be largely a matter of hanging on after others have let go.

— William Feather, 1889 - 1981
American Author

DARING GREATLY

It is not the critic who counts; not the man who points out how the strong man stumbles, or where the doer of deeds could have done better. The credit belongs to the man who is actually in the arena; whose face is marred by dust and sweat and blood; who strives valiantly; who errs and comes short again and again; who knows the great enthusiasms, the great devotions, and spends himself in a worthy cause; who at the best knows in the end the triumph of high achievement; and who at the worst, if he fails, at least fails while daring greatly; so that his place shall never be with those cold and timid souls who neither know victory or defeat.

— Theodore Roosevelt, 1858 - 1919
From the speech, *Citizenship in a Republic,*
(Sorbonne, Paris; April 23, 1910)

• • • • •

If I don't manage to fly, someone else will. The spirit wants only that there be flying. As for who happens to do it, in that he has only a passing interest.

— Rainier Maria Rilke, 1875 - 1926
German Poet

• • • • •

There is only one place you need to go: your own heart. And only one thing you need to do: wake up.

— Yogi Amrit Desai
Doctor of Yoga and Holistic Healing

It is in the nature of revolution, the overturning of an existing order, that at its inception a very small number of people are involved. The process in fact, begins with one person and an idea, an idea that persuades a second, then a third and a fourth, and gathers force until the idea is successfully contradicted, absorbed into conventional wisdom, or actually turns the world upside down. A revolution requires not only ammunition, but also weapons and men willing to use them and willing to be slain in the battle. In an intellectual revolution, there must be ideas and advocates willing to challenge an entire profession, the establishment itself, willing to spend their reputations and careers in spreading the idea through deeds as well as words.

— JUDE WANNISKI, 1936 - 2005
The Way the World Works, (Touchstone Books, 1978)

• • • • •

THE MASTER GAME

Seek above all, for a game worth playing. Such is the advice of the oracle to modern man. Having found the game, play it with intensity — play as if your life and sanity depended on it (they do depend upon it). Follow the example of the French existentialists and flourish a banner bearing the word "engagement." Though nothing means anything and all roads are marked "No Exit," yet move as if your movements had some purpose. If life does not seem to offer a game worth playing, then invent one. For it must be clear, even to the most clouded intelligence, that any game is better than no game.

— ROBERT S. DEROPP, 1913 - 1987
The Master Game, (Delacorte Press, 1968)

COME BACK KIDS

After Fred Astaire's first screen test, a 1922 memo from the MGM testing director said, "Can't act. Slightly bald. Can dance a little." Astaire kept that memo over the fireplace in his Beverly Hills home.

An expert said of famous football coach Vince Lombardi, "He possesses minimal football knowledge. Lacks motivation."

Walt Disney was fired by a newspaper for lacking ideas. He also went bankrupt several times before he built Disneyland.

Beethoven handled the violin awkwardly and preferred playing his own compositions instead of improving his technique. His teacher called him hopeless as a composer.

— Source Unknown

• • • • •

The tragedy of life is not death, but what dies inside us while we live ....

— Norman Cousins, 1915 - 1990
American Editor and Writer

• • • • •

People stumble over the truth from time to time, but most pick themselves up and hurry off as though nothing happened.

— Winston S. Churchill, 1874 - 1965
British Prime Minister

No problem can stand the assault of sustained thinking.

— VOLTAIRE (FRANÇOIS-MARIE AROUET), 1694 - 1778
French Philosopher & Writer

• • • • •

The paying of one's dues is the supposed anecdote to one's decisions in life. It is the cruelty of the ego that dues are never recognized as fully paid.

— PATRICIA M. BROWN, PH.D.

▶ THE WAY OF TRANSFORMATION

The man who, being really on the Way, falls upon hard times in the world will not, as a consequence, turn to that friend who offers him refuge and comfort and encourages his old self to survive. Rather, he will seek out someone who will faithfully and inexorably help him to risk himself, so that he may endure the suffering and pass courageously through it, thus making of it a "raft that leads to the far shore."

Only to the extent that man exposes himself over and over again to annihilation, can that which is indestructible arise within him. In this lies the dignity of daring. Thus, the aim of practice is not to develop an attitude which allows a man to acquire a state of harmony and peace wherein nothing can ever trouble him. On the contrary, practice should teach him to let himself be assaulted, perturbed, moved, insulted, broken and battered — that is to say, it should enable him to dare to let go his futile hankering after harmony, surcease from pain, and a comfortable life in order that he may discover, in doing battle with the forces that oppose him, that which awaits him beyond the world of opposites.

The first necessity is that we should have the courage to face life, and to encounter all that is most perilous in the world. When this is possible, meditation itself becomes the means by which we accept and welcome the demons which arise from the unconscious — a process very different from the practice of concentration on some object as a protection against such forces. Only if we venture repeatedly through zones of annihilation, can our contact with Divine Being, which is beyond annihilation, become firm and stable. The more a man learns whole-heartedly to confront the world that threatens him with isolation, the more are the depths of the Ground of Being revealed and the possibilities of new life and Becoming opened.

— Karlfried Graf von Dürckheim, 1896-1988
The Way of Transformation: Daily Life as a Spiritual Exercise
(Allen & Unwin; London, 1988)

LIFE MASTERY DEFINED

CONFIDENCE.

Seeing it ... Feeling it ... Trusting it.

PEACE.

Knowing yourself. Knowing your path. Trusting it all.

SUCCESS.

Progressing on your chosen path and being in love with the process.

COMMITMENT.

Aligning mind, body and spirit in a singleness of purpose to not be denied.

FUN.

The least expensive way to heal your inner child.

COURAGE.

Seeing the danger and acting anyway.

CREATIVITY.

Making up ... I can do. I will do. I am doing!

ENTHUSIASM.

Your God within. I am sold myself.

HEALTH.

The choice is with or without.

LISTENING.

The greatest gift you can give another.

OPTIMISM.

You can make up a horror flick or a love story. Your choice.

LOVE.

In the end, all we really wanted. Give it now; accept it now.

MONEY.

The choice is with or without.

TIME.

Wasting it is easy until you do not have any left.

LEADERSHIP.

Parting the seas with your Vision so that others may venture out.

VISION.

A masterpiece or a mess. Your choice.

MOTIVATION.

Without it, nothing else works. With it, nothing else matters.

JUST DO IT ... ANYWAY!

— RICHARD B. BROOKE
Founder, High Performance People, LLC.

▶ BLISSBUSINESS.COM

Richard's site is designed to inspire and provide practical tools that will nurture your success and help you achieve your personal and business goals. Richard taps 30 years of experience as a visionary leader, trainer and coach to lead you on a journey of self-fulfillment, personal freedom and financial independence.

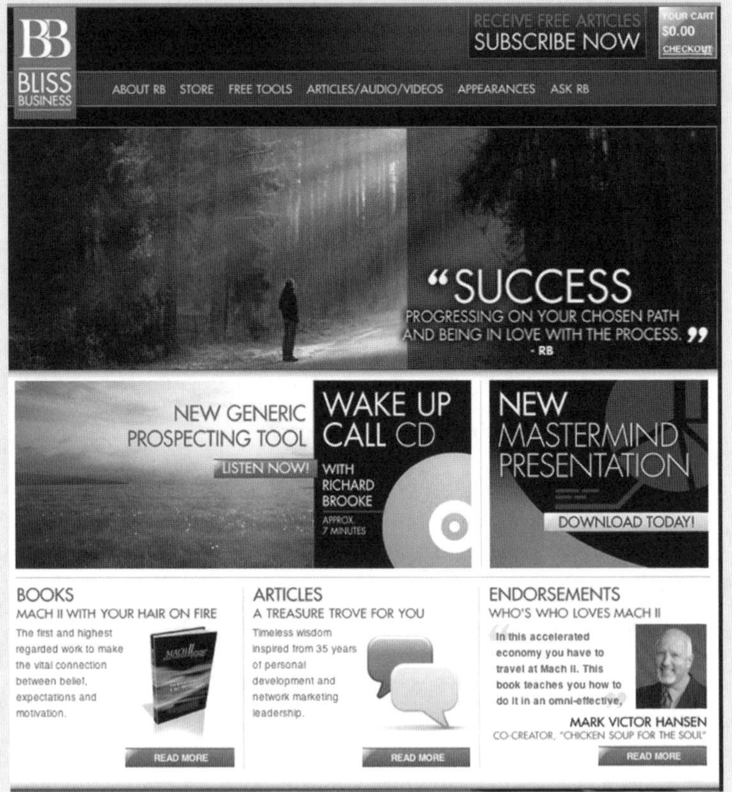

AT BLISSBUSINESS.COM YOU WILL FIND:

- FREE monthly **blog subscription** – Sign up to receive Richard's latest training and send to your friends with a click of your mouse.
- FREE access for downloading dozens of archived **training articles, audios, videos, PowerPoints and books** to your computer and/or iPod!
- FREE **real-time quizzes** that assess your skill level and give you on-the-spot feedback.
- FREE access to Richard himself! Ask your questions and/or **request a guest appearance** on your next group training call.
- **Books, CDs and software** available to order. Get your whole team using them!
- Dates and locations of Richard's next **Vision workshop, seminar or retreat.**
- A brief bio that will leave you eager to read the rest of Richard's story in *Mach II With Your Hair On Fire.*
- Dozens of endorsements hailing the virtues of Richard's tools and trainings.
- A photo gallery that will inspire you to create a lifestyle of choice for yourself!

• • • • •

"If you are committed to extraordinary success, Richard Brooke's information on Vision and Self-Motivation is some of the best you will find anywhere. Richard is a great example of what a person can do with the right information ... plus, he understands the importance of sharing."

BOB PROCTOR
Author of best-selling book, *You Were Born Rich*

NOTES

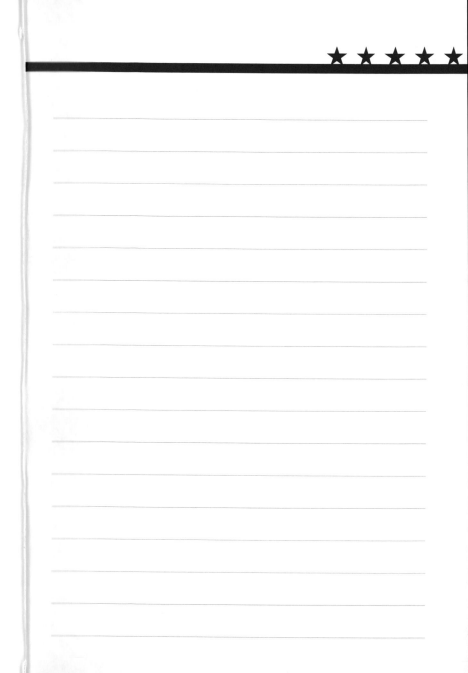